# ★★★★★★★★★★ HARCOURT **HORIZONS**

# TIME FOR KIDS

**Texas Extra!**

# Standing Tall for TEXAS

# Texas Symbols

What symbols stand for Texas?

**Friendship** is the state's motto. Why is friendship important?

United States

Texas

This is the Texas state seal. It is an important symbol for Texas.

This is a map of the United States. The state of Texas is in red.

TIME FOR KIDS Texas Extra!

# Flags Fly

This is the **Texas state flag**.
Have you seen it waving in the breeze?

How many colors are on the flag?

How many stars are on the flag?

RICHARD CUMMINGS/CORBIS

This is the **American flag**.
How is it the same as
the Texas flag?
How is it different?

TIME FOR KIDS **Texas Extra!**

3

# Texas Animals Today

All of the animals on these two pages can be found in Texas.

Clouds of orange fill the Texas sky. The clouds are **monarch butterflies**. They fly across Texas to spend the winter in Mexico.

GARY W. CARTER/CORBIS

DAN GURAVICH/CORBIS

FRANK LANE PICTURE COLLECTION/CORBIS

You can hear sweet tweets from the **mockingbird**. Do you think it can sing "Texas, Our Texas"? That is the Texas state song. Can you sing it?

Horns can be eight feet from end to end.

**Longhorns are large animals. Many live on big ranches in Texas.**

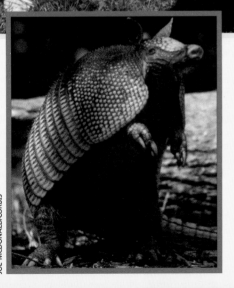

The **armadillo** is a small animal. Armadillos live all over Texas. Have you seen one?

GERALD FRENCH/CORBIS

JOE McDONALD/CORBIS

# Big and Small Plants

The big **prickly pear cactus** grows in Texas. How do you think it got its name?

**Did You Know?**

A prickly pear cactus can be 7 feet tall. A bluebonnet can be 15 inches tall. Is a bluebonnet taller than a cactus?

**Bluebonnets** bloom in spring. They are the state flower.

# Hot Food and Dancing Fun

Many people in Texas love spicy food. **Chili** is the Texas state dish.

JOHN E. KELLY/FOODPIX

The square dance is fun. Do you know how to do any square dances?

OWEN FRANKEN/CORBIS

# Texas Dinosaur

Many kinds of dinosaurs lived where Texas is today. They lived there millions of years ago. One kind of dinosaur was 50 feet tall. That is Texas-size!

## Think Big!

What symbols stand for the United States?

## How Tall?

The pictures below show you the different sizes of some of the things you have read about. Which is the tallest? Which is the shortest? Are you taller than an armadillo?

Mockingbird     Armadillo     Six-year-old     Brachiosaur

TIME FOR KIDS Texas Extra!

# The Pledge of Allegiance

I pledge allegiance to the Flag

of the United States of America,

and to the Republic

for which it stands,

one Nation under God, indivisible,

with liberty and justice for all.

# HARCOURT HORIZONS

# About My World

# ⬅Harcourt

Orlando   Austin   Chicago   New York   Toronto   London   San Diego

Visit *The Learning Site!*
**www.harcourtschool.com**

## General Editor

**Dr. Michael J. Berson**
Associate Professor
Social Science Education
University of South Florida
Tampa, Florida

## Contributing Authors

**Dr. Sherry Field**
Associate Professor
The University of Texas at Austin
Austin, Texas

**Dr. Tyrone Howard**
Assistant Professor
UCLA Graduate School of
    Education & Information Studies
University of California at Los
    Angeles
Los Angeles, California

**Dr. Bruce E. Larson**
Associate Professor of Teacher
    Education and Social Studies
Western Washington University
Bellingham, Washington

## Series Consultants

**Dr. Robert Bednarz**
Professor
Department of Geography
Texas A&M University
College Station, Texas

**Linda McMillan Fields**
Social Studies Supervisor
Spring Branch Independent
    School District
Houston, Texas

**Dr. Asa Grant Hilliard III**
Fuller E. Callaway Professor
    of Urban Education
Georgia State University
Atlanta, Georgia

**Dr. Thomas M. McGowan**
Chairperson and Professor
Center for Curriculum and
    Instruction
University of Nebraska
Lincoln, Nebraska

**Dr. John J. Patrick**
Professor of Education
Indiana University
Bloomington, Indiana

**Dr. Cinthia Salinas**
Assistant Professor
Department of Curriculum and
    Instruction
University of Texas at Austin
Austin, Texas

**Dr. Philip VanFossen**
Associate Professor,
    Social Studies
    Education, and
    Associate Director,
    Purdue Center for Economic
    Education
Purdue University
West Lafayette, Indiana

**Dr. Hallie Kay Yopp**
Professor
Department of
    Elementary, Bilingual,
    and Reading Education
California State
    University, Fullerton
Fullerton, California

**Maps**
researched and prepared by

**Readers**
written and designed by

**Take a Field Trip**
video tour segments provided by

# Contents

· UNIT ·

6

# Jobs People Do

# Reference

# Features You Can Use

# Maps

# Atlas

**A1**

ARCTIC OCEAN

Mackenzie R.

Hudson
Bay

**NORTH
AMERICA**

ROCKY MOUNTAINS

Columbia
R.

Great Lakes

Colorado R.

Missouri R.

Ohio R.

APPALACHIAN MTS.

ATLANTIC
OCEAN

Gulf of
Mexico

PACIFIC
OCEAN

Caribbean Sea

Amazon R.

**SOUTH
AMERICA**

ANDES MOUNTAINS

PACIFIC
OCEAN

Greenland

ARCTIC OCEAN

URAL MTS.

Volga R.

ASIA

EUROPE

Sea of Okhotsk

Black Sea

Caspian Sea

GOBI (DESERT)

Mediterranean Sea

PACIFIC
OCEAN

ATLAS MTS.

HIMALAYAS

Huang He

S A H A R A

Nile R.

Chang Jiang

Ganges R.

Arabian
Sea

AFRICA

Bay of
Bengal

South
China
Sea

Congo  River

Sumatra

Lake Victoria

New
Guinea

Lake
Tanganyika

INDIAN
OCEAN

Madagascar

Kalahari
Desert

AUSTRALIA

GREAT VICTORIA
DESERT

Darling R.

ATLANTIC
OCEAN

Murray
R.

North

West        East

South

ANTARCTICA

A3

ARCTIC OCEAN

NORTH AMERICA

PACIFIC OCEAN

ATLANTIC OCEAN

Equator

SOUTH AMERICA

PACIFIC OCEAN

**A4**

ARCTIC OCEAN

EUROPE

ASIA

PACIFIC OCEAN

AFRICA

INDIAN OCEAN

AUSTRALIA

North

West — East

South

ATLANTIC OCEAN

ANTARCTICA

**A5**

**RUSSIA**

Alaska
**(UNITED STATES)**

*PACIFIC OCEAN*

```
0          250        500 Miles
0      250     500 Kilometers
```

══════ National border

North
West  East
South

Hawaii
**(UNITED STATES)**

ICELAND

Greenland
(DENMARK)

Hudson
Bay

CANADA

Lake Superior

Lake Michigan

Lake Huron

Lake
Ontario

Lake
Erie

Great
Salt Lake

UNITED STATES

ATLANTIC OCEAN

of California

MEXICO

Gulf of Mexico

BAHAMAS

CUBA

DOMINICAN
REPUBLIC

Puerto
Rico
(U.S.)

HAITI

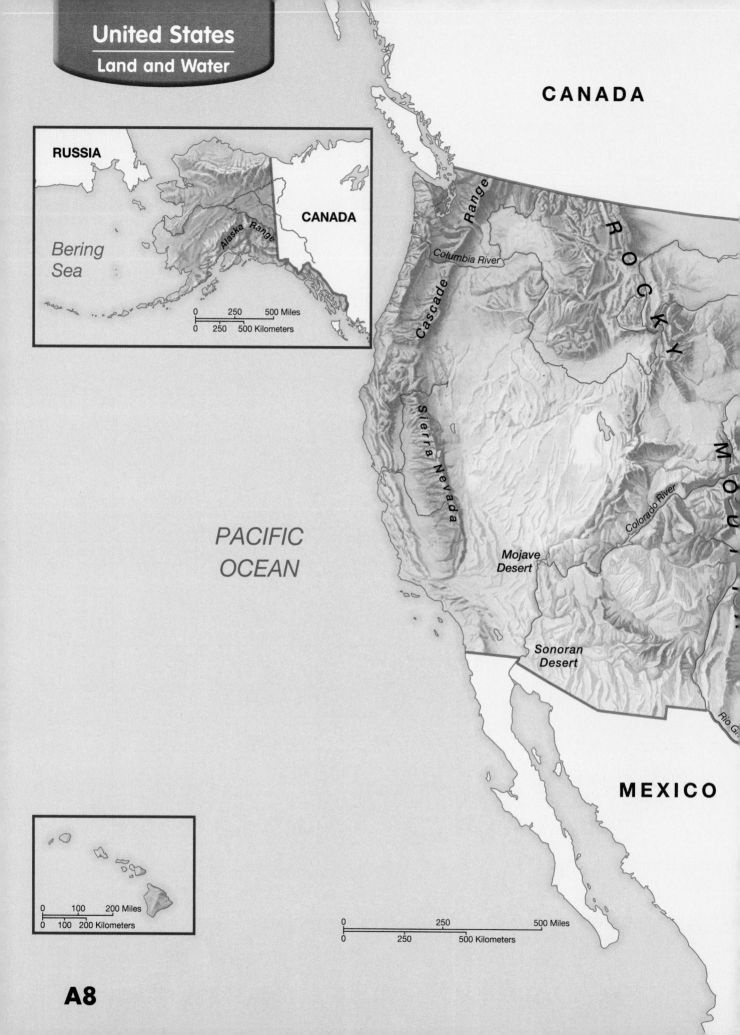

# United States
## Land and Water

**CANADA**

**RUSSIA**

Bering
Sea

*Alaska Range*

**CANADA**

0  250  500 Miles
0  250  500 Kilometers

**ROCKY**

Range

Cascade

*Columbia River*

Sierra Nevada

**M O U N T A I**

*Colorado River*

PACIFIC
OCEAN

*Mojave
Desert*

*Sonoran
Desert*

*Rio Gr*

**MEXICO**

0  100  200 Miles
0  100  200 Kilometers

0  250  500 Miles
0  250  500 Kilometers

**A8**

CANADA

GREAT PLAINS

Missouri River

Mississippi River

Lake Superior

Lake Michigan

Lake Huron

Lake Ontario

Lake Erie

INTERIOR
PLAINS

Missouri River

Ohio River

APPALACHIAN MOUNTAINS

Mississippi River

ATLANTIC
OCEAN

COASTAL    PLAIN

BAHAMAS

Rio Grande

North

West    East

South

Gulf of
Mexico

Straits of Florida

CUBA

A9

CANADA

RUSSIA

ARCTIC OCEAN

ALASKA
(AK)

CANADA

Bering
Sea

PACIFIC OCEAN

WASHINGTON
(WA)

MONTANA
(MT)

OREGON
(OR)

IDAHO
(ID)

WYOMING
(WY)

PACIFIC

OCEAN

NEVADA
(NV)

UTAH
(UT)

COLORADO
(CO)

CALIFORNIA
(CA)

HAWAII
(HI)

PACIFIC
OCEAN

ARIZONA
(AZ)

NEW
MEXICO
(NM)

MEXICO

North

West    East

South

CANADA

Lake Superior

MICHIGAN

Lake Huron

Lake Michigan

Lake Ontario

Lake Erie

NORTH DAKOTA (ND)

MINNESOTA (MN)

SOUTH DAKOTA (SD)

WISCONSIN (WI)

MICHIGAN (MI)

MAINE (ME)

VERMONT (VT)

NEW HAMPSHIRE (NH)

NEW YORK (NY)

MASSACHUSETTS (MA)

RHODE ISLAND (RI)

CONNECTICUT (CT)

NEBRASKA (NE)

IOWA (IA)

ILLINOIS (IL)

INDIANA (IN)

OHIO (OH)

PENNSYLVANIA (PA)

NEW JERSEY (NJ)

MARYLAND (MD)

DELAWARE (DE)

Washington, D.C.

KANSAS (KS)

MISSOURI (MO)

KENTUCKY (KY)

WEST VIRGINIA (WV)

VIRGINIA (VA)

NORTH CAROLINA (NC)

TENNESSEE (TN)

OKLAHOMA (OK)

ARKANSAS (AR)

SOUTH CAROLINA (SC)

GEORGIA (GA)

ATLANTIC

OCEAN

TEXAS (TX)

MISSISSIPPI (MS)

ALABAMA (AL)

LOUISIANA (LA)

FLORIDA (FL)

Gulf of Mexico

CUBA

**A11**

Labels on image: mountain, lake, valley, river, forest, plain, hill, desert, gulf, island, peninsula, ocean

**desert** a large, dry area of land

**forest** a large area of trees

**gulf** a large body of ocean water that is partly surrounded by land

**hill** land that rises above the land around it

**island** a landform with water all around it

**lake** a body of water with land on all sides

**mountain** highest kind of land

**ocean** a body of salt water that covers a large area

**peninsula** a landform that is surrounded on only three sides by water

**plain** flat land

**river** a large stream of water that flows across the land

**valley** low land between hills or mountains

# Going to School

Eagle on Uncle Sam's Hat
Tradesign, 1870

# Going to School

**❝ Enter to Learn
Depart to Serve ❞**

—signs entering and leaving Mary McLeod Bethune's school in Daytona Beach, Florida, 1914

## Preview the Content

Make a table to show how schools around the world are alike and different. As you read this unit, add to the table. Show what you learn about school workers, ways you learn, and tools you use.

| Schools | |
|---|---|
| Alike | Different |
|  |  |

**learn** To find out something new. (page 6)

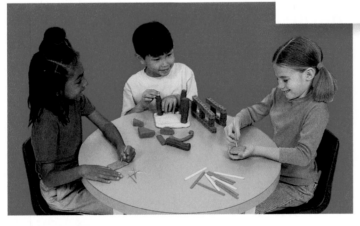

**rule** An instruction telling what must or must not be done. (page 10)

**group** A number of people working together. (page 12)

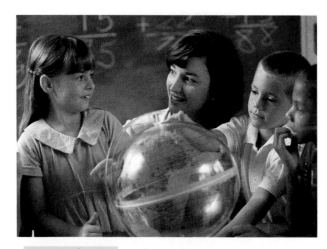

**teacher** A person who helps others learn. (page 14)

**principal** The leader of a school. (page 14)

# School Bus

by Lee Bennett Hopkins
illustrated by Lori Lohstoeter

This wide-awake
freshly-painted-yellow
school bus

readied for Fall

carries us all—

Sixteen boys—
Fourteen girls—

Thirty pairs of sleepy eyes

and

hundreds
upon
hundreds

of

school supplies.

# Think About It

1. What does the poem tell you about these children?

2. How do you get ready for school?

## Read a Book

## Start the Unit Project

**A Classroom Scrapbook** Your class will start a scrapbook. As you read this unit, draw and write about the new things you learn.

## Use Technology

Visit The Learning Site at **www.harcourtschool.com/ socialstudies** for additional activities, primary sources, and other resources to use in this unit.

# 1 Going to School

**1. lesson number**

**2. title**

**Main Idea**
School is a place to learn and share.

**Vocabulary**

learn

share

**3. new word**

Our school is where we learn. When we **learn**, we find out something new. We read at school to learn. We write, draw, and tell stories, too.

Our school is where we share. We **share** what we know and who we are.

4. picture

5. question

1 **Vocabulary**    What do you want to **learn** in school?

2 What do the pictures tell you about how children in this classroom learn?

3 Draw a picture of something you did today in school.

# Find the Main Idea

**Vocabulary**

main idea

detail

## ▶ Why It Matters

The **main idea** tells you what you are reading about.

## ▶ What You Need to Know

A paragraph has a main idea. Paragraphs also have detail sentences. A **detail** gives more information. Details help explain the main idea.

## ▶ Practice the Skill

❶ Read the paragraph on page 9. What is the main idea?

❷ What is one detail in the paragraph?

**Braille watch**

## Braille

People who cannot see can use the Braille alphabet to read and write. Groups of small, raised dots stand for letters in the alphabet. Other groups of dots stand for numbers. The dot letters spell out words. People who are blind read the words by running their fingers along the dots. ■

▶ **Apply What You Learned**

Read a children's magazine article. Look for main ideas and details.

# Rules at School

**Main Idea**
Good rules are fair and help people work together.

We have rules in our classroom. A **rule** tells what you must do. Rules help us work and play safely.

Class Rules
- Talk quietly.
- Take turns.
- Follow directions.
- Be kind.

Rules help us listen, share, and work together in a fair way. **Fair** means acting in a way that is right and honest.

Follow the rules.

**LESSON 2**
**Review**

1. **Vocabulary** How do **rules** help people be **fair**?

2. Explain why we need rules at school.

3. Choose a school rule. Draw a picture of children following that rule.

# Working Together

**Vocabulary**

group

## ▶ Why It Matters

In school, children may work alone or with others in a **group**. People in a group need to know how to work together.

## ▶ What You Need to Know

These steps help group members work together.

**Step 1** Plan together.

**Step 2** Act together.

**Step 3** Think about how well your group worked together.

❶ Study the picture.

❷ Work in a group to write rules the children in this playground can use.

## ▶ Apply What You Learned

Work with family members to plan an activity. Use the steps you learned.

# School Workers

**Main Idea**
There are many workers at a school.

**Vocabulary**
teacher
principal

Our school has many workers. Our **teacher** helps us learn. Our **principal** helps make our school a safe place.

teacher

principal

## Mary McLeod Bethune

**1875–1955**

**Character Trait: Perseverance**

When Mary McLeod Bethune was young, there were few schools for African American children. When she found one, she worked hard and became a teacher. She later opened a school and then a college where African Americans could go to learn.

MULTIMEDIA BIOGRAPHIES
Visit The Learning Site at
**www.harcourtschool.com/biographies**
to learn about other famous people.

15

How are these school
workers helping?

nurse

custodian

teacher aide

librarian

food server

1 **Vocabulary** How does a **teacher** help children?

2 How do you help at school?

3 Make a list of people who help you at school. Write a thank-you card for a worker from your list.

17

# Where Are You?

The **location** of a place is where the place is. The drawing shows where the rooms are in this school. Describe the location of each room. Use words such as <u>next to</u>, <u>beside</u>, and <u>across from</u>.

GEOGRAPHY THEME

Which room is between the music room and the gym?

**LESSON 4**
**Review**

1. **Vocabulary** Describe the **location** of the music room.

2. How is this school like your school?

3. Imagine you are helping a child who is new to your school. Describe the location of rooms he or she might need to find.

## Skills

MAP AND GLOBE

# Looking at Maps

Vocabulary

map

symbol

## ▶ Why It Matters

A **map** is a drawing that shows where places are. Maps help you find places.

## ▶ What You Need to Know

Mapmakers use **symbols**, or pictures, to stand for real things.

playground

music room

cafeteria

gym

classroom

office

library

# Practice the Skill

**1** Look at the map. Where is the playground? How do you know?

**2** What rooms are next to the cafeteria?

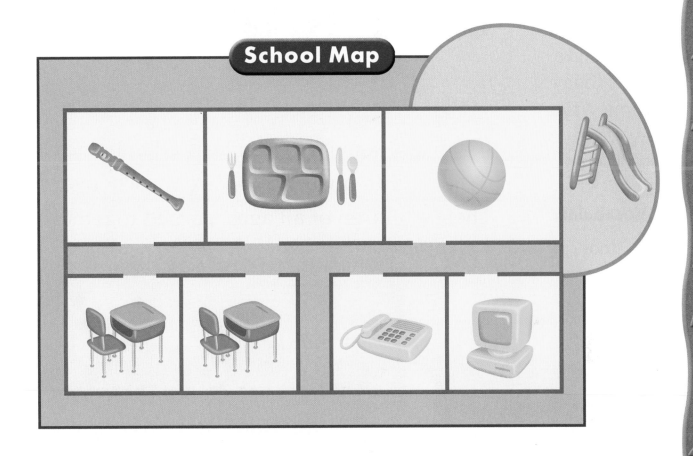

**School Map**

# Apply What You Learned

Make a map of your classroom. Use symbols to show where things are in the room.

Practice your map and globe skills with the **GeoSkills CD-ROM.**

# 5

## Schools Long Ago and Today

**Main Idea**
Schools long ago were like schools today in some ways. They were also different.

**Vocabulary**

tool

### Then

Long ago, some children learned at home. Other children went to one-room schools. There, children of all ages learned together.

# Now

Some ways of learning are the same today as they were long ago. Some ways are different. Today there are many more kinds of schools.

Hebrew school

Special-needs school

Home school

Multiage class

23

# Then

A **tool** is something people use. Some tools are used for learning. Long ago, children had few tools.

An abacus is a very old tool used for counting. Today most people use a calculator, but some people still use an abacus.

# Now

Today children use many tools to learn.

① **Vocabulary** What **tools** do you use in school?

② How were schools different long ago?

③ Write three sentences that describe your school.

# Put Things into Groups

| Vocabulary |
| --- |
| table |

## ▶ Why It Matters

Putting things into groups helps you see how they are alike and different.

## ▶ What You Need to Know

A **table** is a chart that shows things in groups. Labels tell you what is in each group.

## ▶ Practice the Skill

1 Look at the chart. Which side shows tools from long ago? Which side shows tools from today?

2 What did children use to write with long ago? What do they use today?

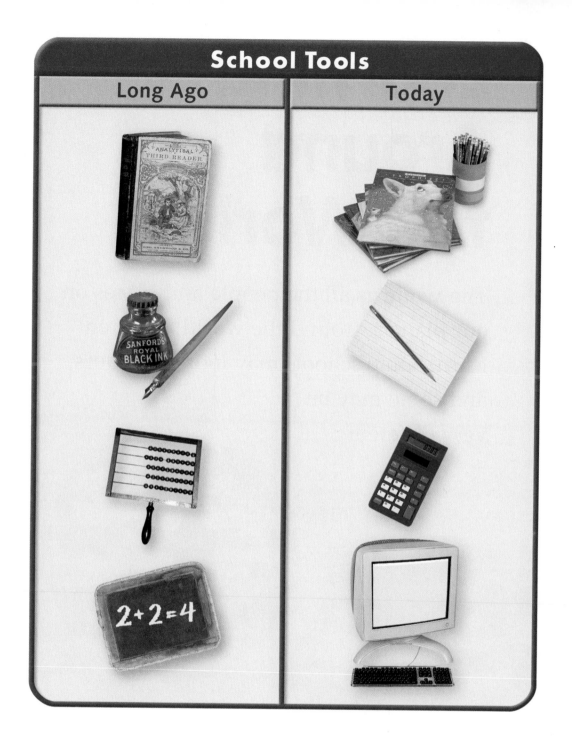

## School Tools

| Long Ago | Today |
|---|---|

## ▶ Apply What You Learned

Make a table that shows Reading Tools and Writing Tools. Use the tools on the Today side of the table on this page to make your new table.

**Main Idea**
Schools around the world are the same in many ways.

# Learning Around the World

The **world** is all the people and places on our planet. Around the world, children learn. Some schools may look like yours, and some may be very different.

Germany

Mexico

## The Internet

The Internet makes it easy for people to learn and share. With this tool, you can find information about many things. You can see art in a museum far away. You can even send messages around the world.

Togo

Brazil

31

Some learning
happens outside
of the classroom.
How are these
children learning?

**Venezuela**

**Japan**

**Egypt**

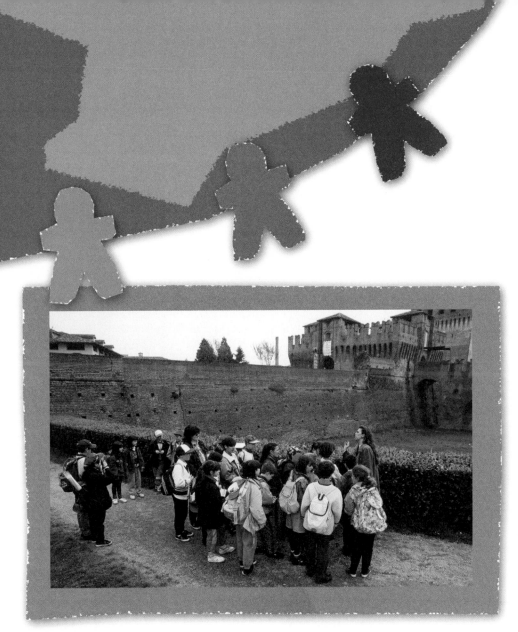

**Italy**

❶ **Vocabulary** What is the **world**?

❷ How are the ways these children learn the same as the ways you learn?

❸ Write a letter telling someone far away about your school.

# A School for Firefighters

## Get Ready

There are many kinds of schools. At a school for firefighters, people learn how to fight fires and keep others safe. They also learn how to work together as a team.

## What to See

Students help each other use a fire hose.

Students practice using a ladder.

There is a lot to learn about the fire truck.

The water hose hooks up to the fire hydrant.

Students study fire safety rules.

## Take a Field Trip

**GO ONLINE**

**A VIRTUAL TOUR**
Visit The Learning Site at **www.harcourtschool.com/tours** to take virtual tours of other kinds of schools.

**A VIDEO TOUR**
**READING RAINBOW** Check your media center or classroom library for a video featuring a segment from Reading Rainbow.

**Visual Summary**

Finish the table to show how schools are alike and different.

| Schools | |
|---|---|
| **Alike** | **Different** |
| Schools have teachers. | Schools are different sizes. |
| Everyone uses tools to learn. | Some classrooms have computers. |
| | |
| | |

## THINK  & WRITE

**Make a Choice** Choose a tool you use every day in school.

**Write a Label** Write the name of the tool. Tell how it is used.

## Use Vocabulary

Write the word that goes with each meaning.

**1** a number of people working together

**2** the leader of a school

**3** an instruction telling what must be done

**4** a person who helps others learn

**5** to find out something new

learn
(p. 6)
**rule**
(p. 10)
**group**
(p. 12)
**teacher**
(p. 14)
**principal**
(p. 14)

## Recall Facts

**6** Name a school rule that helps children be fair.

**7** What tools help you learn?

**8** Tell two ways schools today are different from schools long ago.

**9** Which of these school workers helps you find a book?

**A** nurse        **C** custodian

**B** librarian      **D** food server

**10** Which of these is a good symbol for a cafeteria?

**F**

**G**

**H**

**J**

**11** What can happen when people do not follow rules?

**12** How is working in a group different from working alone?

## Apply Chart and Graph Skills

| Rules | |
|---|---|
| **School Rules** | **Home Rules** |
| Raise hand | Make bed |
| Stand in line | Feed fish |
| Hang up backpack | Keep room clean |

**13** What is the title of this table?

**14** Which side shows rules at school? Which side shows rules at home?

**15** Is **Feed fish** a school or home rule?

**16** On which side would the rule **Take turns** go?

Study these symbols.

| Art center | Child's desk | Lunch boxes | Reading corner | Teacher's desk |

**Joe's Classroom**

⓱ What does this map show?

⓲ What is the symbol for the reading corner?

⓳ What is the brush a symbol for?

⓴ What is between the art center and the reading corner?

# Unit Activities

**GO ONLINE**

Visit The Learning Site at
www.harcourtschool.com/
socialstudies/activities
for additional activities.

**Complete the Unit Project** Work with your group to finish the unit project. Decide what you want to show in your scrapbook. Make a cover.

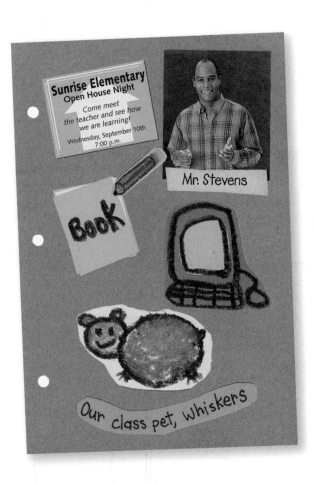

Sunrise Elementary
Open House Night
Come meet the teacher and see how we are learning!
Wednesday, September 10th
7:00 p.m.

Mr. Stevens

Book

Our class pet, Whiskers

## Choose a Place

Choose one of these places in your school. Draw a picture of it.
- classroom
- cafeteria
- library

## Match Workers and Tools

Draw pictures of school workers. Find or draw pictures of the tools they use at work. Match the workers to their tools.

## Visit Your Library

**Get Up and Go!** by Stuart J. Murphy. Follow a young girl as she gets ready for school on a busy morning.

**First Day, Hooray!** by Nancy Poydar. Workers and students are getting ready for the first day of school.

**A School Album** by Peter and Connie Roop. See how schools long ago and today are alike and different.

# Good Citizens

An airplane hood ornament
for car, 1915

# 2

# Good Citizens

**"I pledge allegiance to my flag."**

—Francis Bellamy, in the magazine *Youth's Companion*, September 8, 1892

## Preview the Content

Make a chart to show what you know and what you want to know about being a good citizen. At the end of this unit, finish the chart with what you learned.

| K-W-L Chart | | |
|---|---|---|
| What I Know | What I Want to Know | What I Learned |
| | | |

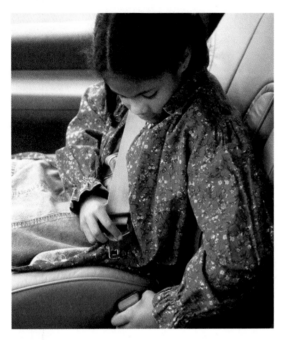

**law** A rule that people in a community must follow. (page 46)

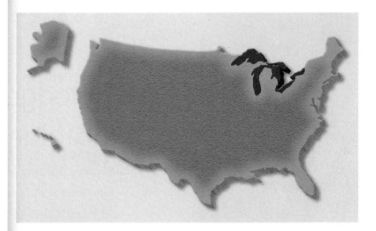

**country** An area of land with its own people and laws. (page 52)

**state** A part of a country. (page 52)

**President** The leader of the United States government. (page 54)

**flag** A piece of cloth with a special design that stands for a country or group. (page 62)

**citizen** A person who lives in and belongs to a community. (page 68)

# America

**by Samuel F. Smith**
**illustrated by Erika LeBarre**

My country, 'tis of thee,
Sweet land of liberty,
Of thee I sing.
Land where my fathers died,
Land of the Pilgrims' pride,
From every mountainside
Let freedom ring!

My native country, thee,
Land of the noble free,
Thy name I love.
I love thy rocks and rills,
Thy woods and templed hills;
My heart with rapture thrills
Like that above.

# Think About It

1. What does the author tell us about America?

2. How does the song make you feel?

## Read a Book

## Start the Unit Project

**Proud Citizens Mobile** Your class will make a mobile that shows people being proud citizens. As you read this unit, think about how we show pride in our community, state, and country.

## Use Technology

Visit The Learning Site at **www.harcourtschool.com/ socialstudies** for additional activities, primary sources, and other resources to use in this unit.

45

# Rules and Laws

A community has rules called laws. A **law** is a rule that people in a community must follow. A **community** is a group of people who live or work together. It is also the place where those people live.

Police officers work to keep people safe.
They make sure that people obey the laws.

**LESSON 1**
**Review**

1 **Vocabulary** Explain why **communities** need **laws**.

2 How are rules and laws the same? How are they different?

3 Make a sign for a law in your community that helps keep people safe.

# Who Are Our Leaders?

**Main Idea**
Leaders help people follow rules and laws.

**Vocabulary**

leader

mayor

city

governor

government

You belong to many groups. You are a member of a family, a class, and a school. Most groups have leaders. A **leader** is in charge of helping a group of people follow rules.

P.T.A.
MEETING
7:30 P.
m C-5

Communities also have leaders. A **mayor** is the leader of a city or town. A **city** is a large, busy community. A mayor works with other leaders to make a community a good place to live.

Mayor
Stephen Luecke
of South Bend,
Indiana

A **governor** is also a leader. The governor works for many communities.

Mayors and governors are part of the government. The **government** is a group of people who make laws. Government workers also do other jobs in a community, such as repairing roads, keeping parks in good condition, and helping when there is a fire.

Work with your leaders.

**LESSON 2**
**Review**

1 **Vocabulary** What do **leaders** do?

2 How can you help leaders at school and in the community?

3 Pretend you are the leader of a group. Tell how you would help the group members.

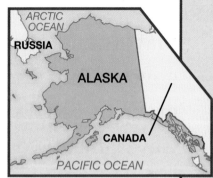

# Skills

**MAP AND GLOBE**

# Find States on a Map

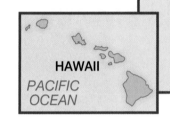

| Vocabulary |
| :---: |
| country |
| state |
| border |

## ▶ Why It Matters

A **country** is an area of land with its own people and laws. Our country is the United States of America. The United States is made up of 50 states. A **state** is one part of our country.

## ▶ What You Need to Know

On a map, lines called borders separate states and countries. A **border** shows where a state or country ends. The countries of Canada and Mexico have borders that touch the United States.

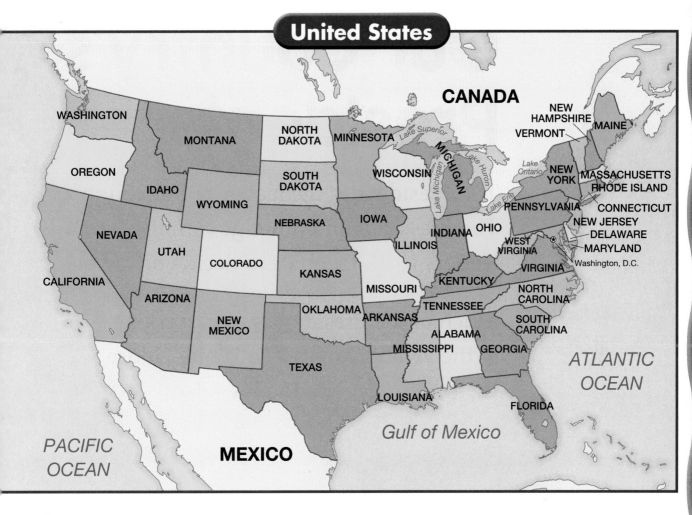

**United States**

WASHINGTON
MONTANA
NORTH DAKOTA
MINNESOTA
CANADA
Lake Superior
NEW HAMPSHIRE
VERMONT
MAINE
OREGON
IDAHO
SOUTH DAKOTA
WISCONSIN
MICHIGAN
Lake Huron
Lake Ontario
NEW YORK
MASSACHUSETTS
RHODE ISLAND
WYOMING
NEBRASKA
IOWA
Lake Michigan
Lake Erie
PENNSYLVANIA
CONNECTICUT
NEVADA
NEW JERSEY
UTAH
COLORADO
INDIANA
OHIO
ILLINOIS
WEST VIRGINIA
DELAWARE
MARYLAND
CALIFORNIA
ARIZONA
KANSAS
MISSOURI
KENTUCKY
VIRGINIA
Washington, D.C.
NEW MEXICO
OKLAHOMA
ARKANSAS
TENNESSEE
NORTH CAROLINA
SOUTH CAROLINA
TEXAS
MISSISSIPPI
ALABAMA
GEORGIA
ATLANTIC OCEAN
LOUISIANA
FLORIDA
PACIFIC OCEAN
MEXICO
Gulf of Mexico

## ▶ Practice the Skill

**1** Which state shares a border with Maine?

**2** Locate your state. Name a state that is near yours.

**3** How many states share Virginia's border?

## ▶ Apply What You Learned

List the states with borders that touch Canada or Mexico.

Practice your map and globe skills with the **GeoSkills CD-ROM.**

# Our Country's Presidents

**Main Idea**
The President is the leader of our country.

**Vocabulary**

President

The **President** is the leader of our country. The President and other government leaders work together to decide on laws.

Much of the President's work is done at the White House. The White House is also the home of the President.

The President meets with people and leaders from around our country. The President visits leaders in other countries, too.

**The White House**

George Washington was the first President of the United States of America. He did not live in the White House, but he helped decide where to build it.

George Washington was the first person to sign the Constitution of the United States. The Constitution is the plan for our country's government. Our country still follows this plan today.

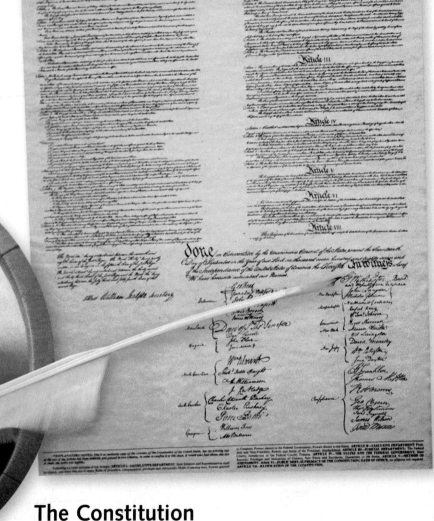

**The Constitution of the United States of America**

## Thomas Jefferson
### 1743–1826
### Character Trait: Responsibility

Thomas Jefferson was the third President of our country. In 1776 he helped write the Declaration of Independence, which started the United States.

**GO ONLINE**

MULTIMEDIA BIOGRAPHIES
Visit The Learning Site at
**www.harcourtschool.com/biographies**
to learn about other famous people.

The Constitution says that Americans can choose who will be President. Our country has had 43 Presidents.

**LESSON 3 Review**

1. **Vocabulary** Who is our country's **President** now?

2. What makes a good President?

3. Draw and write to show something you know about our President.

# Make a Choice by Voting

**Vocabulary**

vote

ballot

## ▶ Why It Matters

Americans vote for many government leaders. When you **vote**, you make a choice. Americans also vote to make choices about laws.

## ▶ What You Need to Know

Americans use a **ballot** to vote. A ballot is a paper that shows all of the choices. You mark on it what your choice is. When voting time is over, the votes for each choice are counted. The choice with the most votes wins.

Ballot
Mr. Garcia's Class

To vote, fill in the arrow to your choice, like this: ◀━ ◀━ pointing

Para votar, complete la flecha a la selección de la siguiente manera: ◀━ ◀━ que apunta

**Class Leader**
**Líder de la clase**

(Vote for One)  (Vote por uno)

Samuel

Teresa ◀━ ◀━

Olivia ◀━ ◀━

**58**

# ▶ Practice the Skill

**1** Mr. Garcia's class used ballots to vote for a class leader. The choices were Samuel, Teresa, and Olivia. The votes were counted. Look at the chart to see who got the most votes.

**2** Who will be the class leader?

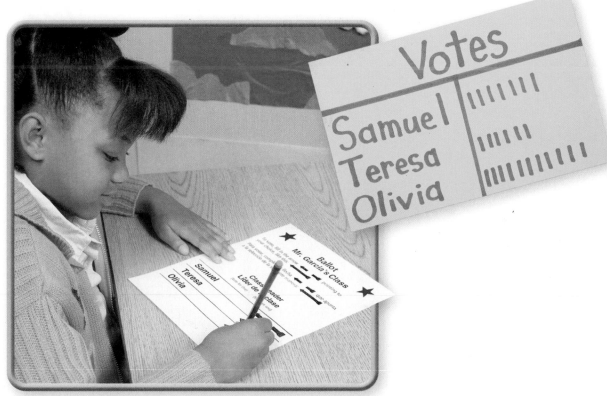

# ▶ Apply What You Learned

Have a class vote. Make a list of books your class would like to read. Make a ballot showing all of the choices. Count the votes each book gets. Show the counts on a chart. Which book does your class most want to read?

# America's Symbols

**Main Idea**
Symbols remind us to show respect for our country.

**Vocabulary**

flag

The United States of America has symbols that remind us of important people and events. Some of these symbols are places we can visit.

**Bald eagle**

**Capitol building**

FAST FACT
A leader named Benjamin Franklin wanted the turkey to be a symbol of the United States. The bald eagle was chosen instead.

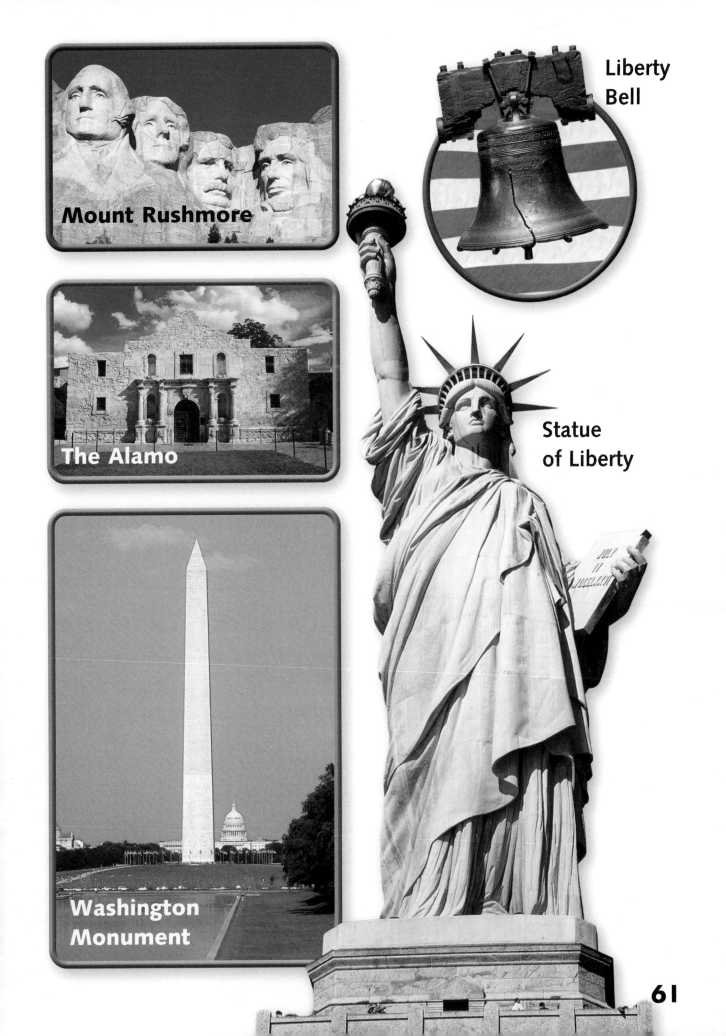

Mount Rushmore

The Alamo

Washington Monument

Liberty Bell

Statue of Liberty

Our **flag** is a symbol of our country. It is red, white, and blue. Each star stands for one of the states in our country. The stripes stand for the first 13 states in the United States. When we say the Pledge of Allegiance, we show that our country is important to us.

# The Pledge of Allegiance

I pledge allegiance to the Flag
of the United States of America,
and to the Republic
for which it stands,
one Nation under God, indivisible,
with liberty and justice for all.

Each state has its own flag.

Some states have pledges to their flags.

Honor the Texas flag.
I pledge allegiance to thee,
Texas, one and indivisible.

I Salute
the Arkansas Flag
With Its Diamond and Stars.
We Pledge
Our Loyalty to Thee.

Our country has the motto, or saying, "In God We Trust." States have mottoes, too.

Pennsylvania

**Virtue, Liberty, and Independence**

Texas

**Friendship**

Indiana

**The Crossroads of America**

**Washington State**

The state of Washington was named for George Washington, the first President of the United States. It is the only state named for a President.

64

We can sing songs that show how proud we
are of our country and our state.

① **Vocabulary** Explain how the **flag** is a symbol for our country.

② Do you think symbols are important? Why?

③ Make a poster to show symbols of your state.

# Fiction or Nonfiction

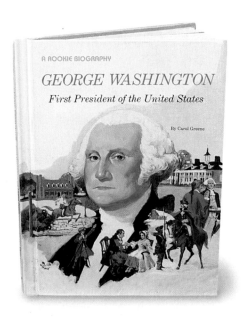

## ▶ Why It Matters

Stories can be made up or real.
Made-up stories are **fiction**. Books
of real information are **nonfiction**.
Nonfiction books tell only facts.
A **fact** is something that is true.

## ▶ What You Need to Know

The title, pictures, and words of a book
let you know if it's fiction or nonfiction.

Then, in 1789,
George was elected
the first president
of the United States.

He didn't think
he was good enough
to be president.
But he took the job.

# Practice the Skill

1. Look at the two books.

2. Which book do you think is fiction? What makes you think so?

3. Which book do you think tells more facts? What makes you think so?

# Apply What You Learned

Choose a book, and look at the cover and the pictures. Do you think the book is fiction or nonfiction? How can you tell?

# Portraits of Good Citizens

**Main Idea**
Good citizens help others.

**Vocabulary**

citizen

A **citizen** is a person who lives in and belongs to a community. Good citizens do things to help people. Read about the ways these good citizens helped others.

## Patriotism

### Nathan Hale
1755–1776
Character Trait: Patriotism

Nathan Hale showed great patriotism, or love for his country. He was a leader who helped Americans fight to be free from the country of England.

# Responsibility

## Sam Houston
**1793–1863**
**Character Trait: Responsibility**

When Sam Houston moved to Texas, it belonged to Mexico. He helped when the Americans living there fought to be free from Mexico. He also worked to make Texas part of the United States.

# Compassion

## Clara Barton
**1821–1912**
**Character Trait: Compassion**

Clara Barton started the American Red Cross. The Red Cross is a group that helps when something bad happens, such as a flood. It gives people food, clothing, and a place to stay.

# Fairness

## Eleanor Roosevelt
### 1884–1962
### Character Trait: Fairness

Eleanor Roosevelt believed that everyone should be treated fairly. She worked with leaders of other countries to help people all over the world have better lives.

# Inventiveness

## Stephanie Kwolek
### born in 1923
### Character Trait: Inventiveness

Stephanie Kwolek made an important new fabric. This material is light but stronger than steel. It is used in the special vests police officers wear. Her discovery has helped save many lives.

# Civic Virtue

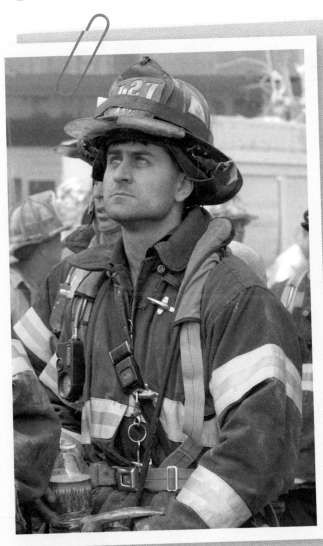

## Firefighters
### Character Trait: Civic Virtue

Some citizens have dangerous jobs. When firefighters are called to work, they do all they can to help people. They will even give up their own safety.

**Many firefighters lost their lives when buildings in New York City were attacked on September 11, 2001.**

---

**LESSON 5**
**Review**

❶ **Vocabulary** What are some ways people can be good **citizens**?

❷ What are some character traits of good citizens?

❸ Think about a good citizen you know. Tell the class about him or her.

# Rights and Responsibilities

**Main Idea**
Citizens have rights and responsibilities.

**Vocabulary**
right
responsibility

Citizens of our country have special rights. A **right** is something people are free to do. They can choose their leaders. They can belong to groups. They can live where they want to live.

**Freedom of religion**

**Freedom of speech**

When people have rights, they also have responsibilities. A **responsibility** is something you should take care of or do. One responsibility is to obey laws. This keeps the community safe.

IT'S THE LAW
clean up after your dog
maximum fine $100
public health law 1310
DEPARTMENT OF SANITATION

**LESSON 6**
**Review**

1. **Vocabulary** What is one **right** that Americans have?

2. What responsibilities do you have at school?

3. Draw a picture that shows a responsibility you have at home.

# How Communities Honor Their Citizens

## Get Ready

Many communities celebrate people who have done something special. They may name a street, park, or building for such a person.

## What to See

This school is named for the poet Gwendolyn Brooks. She wrote poems about people in her neighborhood.

This mural is about the work of architect Daniel Burnham. He planned parks and buildings that gave cities a special look.

PASTEUR PARK
CHICAGO PARK DISTRICT

Pasteur Park is named for a scientist. Louis Pasteur found a way to kill germs in food we eat.

## Take a Field Trip

**GO ONLINE**

**A VIRTUAL TOUR**
Visit The Learning Site at **www.harcourtschool.com/tours** to take virtual tours of other monuments and memorials.

**READING RAINBOW.**

**A VIDEO TOUR**
Check your media center or classroom library for a video featuring a segment from Reading Rainbow.

**Visual Summary**

Finish the chart to show what you have learned about being a good citizen.

### K-W-L Chart

| What I Know | What I Want to Know | What I Learned |
|---|---|---|
| We have laws. | Does everyone have to follow laws? | |
| We have a President. | Who is our President? | |

THINK & WRITE

**Talk About It** Think about some of the symbols of our country. Talk about what the symbols mean.

**Write a Sentence** Choose a symbol. Write a sentence telling why it is a good symbol for our country.

## Use Vocabulary

Write the word that goes with each picture.

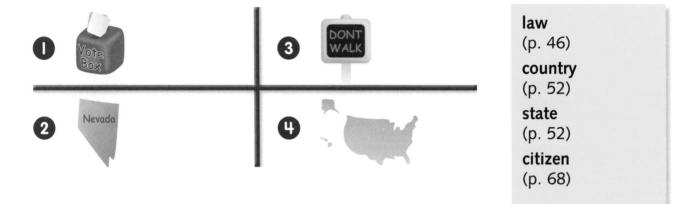

**law**
(p. 46)

**country**
(p. 52)

**state**
(p. 52)

**citizen**
(p. 68)

## Recall Facts

**5** What is a law?

**6** Name leaders in your community and state.

**7** How are a country and a state different?

**8** Who was the first President of the United States?

**9** Which of these is the home of the President of the United States?

　**A** Capitol building　　**C** Alamo

　**B** Washington Monument　**D** White House

**10** Which of these tells about nonfiction books?

　**F** tell no facts　　**H** have real information

　**G** have no pictures　**J** have made-up stories

**11** How do leaders help citizens?

**12** What are some things that good citizens do?

**Apply Chart and Graph Skills**

| Class Field Trip Votes | |
|---|---|
| museum | IIII |
| zoo | IIIIIIIIIII |
| park | IIIIIIII |

**13** What are the children in Mrs. Johnson's class voting about?

**14** What are the choices?

**15** How many votes does the museum have?

**16** Which choice has the most votes?

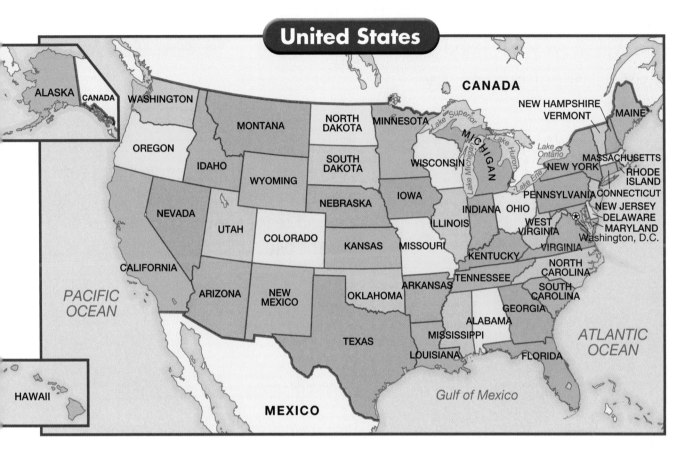

United States

17 Find Indiana. Name the states that share borders with Indiana.

18 What countries share borders with the United States?

19 Which state is closer to Canada, Montana or North Carolina?

20 Which state shares a border with Nebraska, Iowa or Texas?

# Unit Activities

**GO ONLINE**

Visit The Learning Site at
www.harcourtschool.com/
socialstudies/activities
for additional activities.

**Complete the Unit Project** Work with your group to finish the unit project. Decide how you will show what good citizens do and what is special about our country.

Coach Lucy helps players get along

Virginia

Washington, D.C.

## Choose a Leader

Draw one of these leaders. Write a sentence telling why he or she is a good leader. Add your leader to the mobile.
- teacher
- principal
- coach

## American Symbols

Draw or find pictures of American symbols. You can also use your state's symbols. Add the symbols to the mobile.

## Visit Your Library

**The Inside-Outside Book of Washington, D.C.** by Roxie Munro. Take a look at some of the important buildings in Washington, D.C.

**If I Were President** by Catherine Stier. Read about what some children would do if they were President of the United States.

**The Flag We Love** by Pam Muñoz Ryan. Find out facts about the flag of the United States.

# The Land Around Us

PORTABLE
TERRESTRIAL GLOBE.

A folding
pop-up globe

# 3

# The Land Around Us

66 Enjoy the earth gently
Enjoy the earth gently
For if the earth is spoiled
It cannot be repaired
Enjoy the earth gently. 99

—Yoruba (African) song

## Preview the Content

Make a web to show some of our world's natural resources. As you read this unit, add to the web. Write what you learn about Earth's land, water, and other resources.

**neighborhood** The part of a community in which a group of people lives. (page 94)

**continent** One of seven main land areas on Earth. (page 105)

82

**ocean** A very large body of salty water. (page 105)

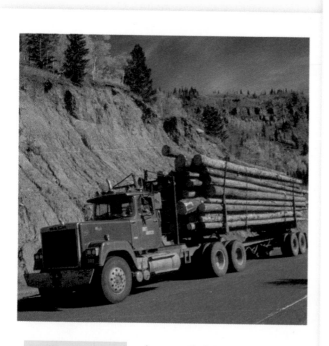

**resource** Anything people can use. (page 108)

**weather** What the air outside is like. (page 112)

**83**

# From Here to There

by Margery Cuyler

illustrated by Yu Cha Pak

People often use their **address** to tell where they live. In this book, Maria describes where she lives in a special way.

My name is Maria Mendoza. I live with my
father, my mother, my baby brother, Tony,
and my older sister, Angelica,

at number 43 Juniper Street—

in the town of Splendora,

**in the county of Montgomery,**

**in the state of Texas,**

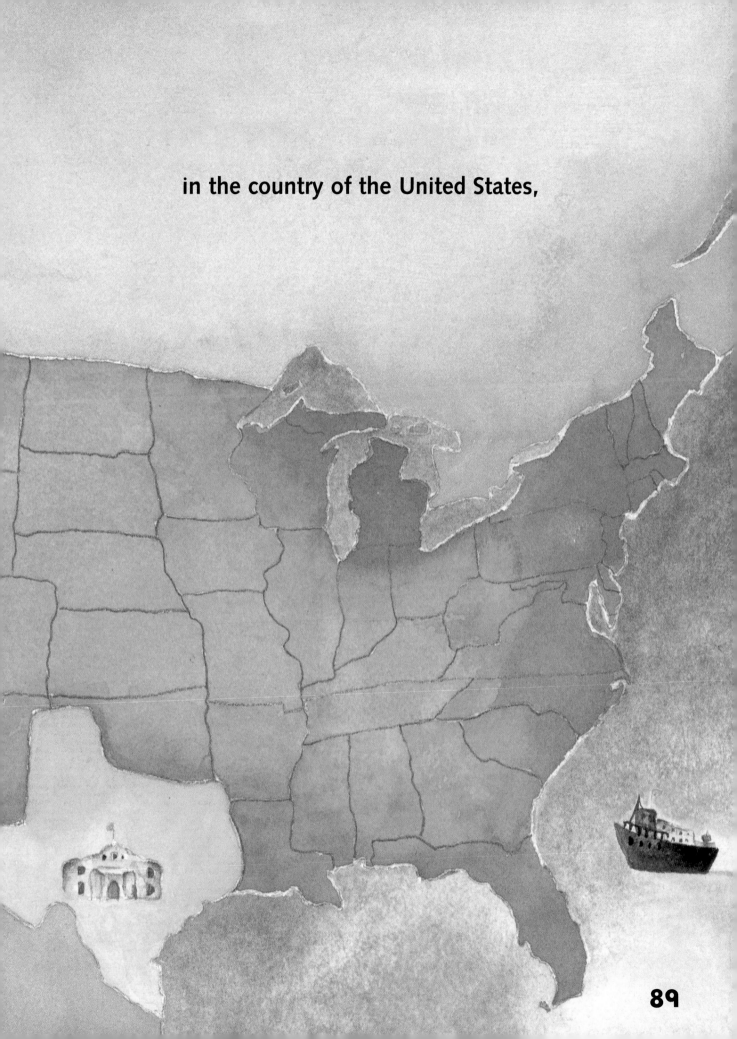

in the country of the United States,

on the continent of North America,

in the Western Hemisphere,

on the planet Earth,
in the solar system,

in the Milky Way galaxy,
in the universe
and beyond.

From here to there,
my name is
Maria Mendoza.

# Think About It

1 How does Maria describe
   where she lives?

2 Write your address on
   an envelope.

## Read a Book

## Start the Unit Project

**A Community Collage** Your
class will make a collage to
show the kinds of land, water,
and resources in and around
your community. As you read
this unit, remember how these
things are important.

## Use Technology

Visit The Learning Site at
**www.harcourtschool.com/
socialstudies** for additional
activities, primary sources,
and other resources to use
in this unit.

# A Neighborhood

Not far from Splendora, where Maria lives, is the city of Houston. Houston is a large community with many neighborhoods. A **neighborhood** is a small part of a community in which people live. People in a neighborhood share schools, libraries, parks, and other places of the community.

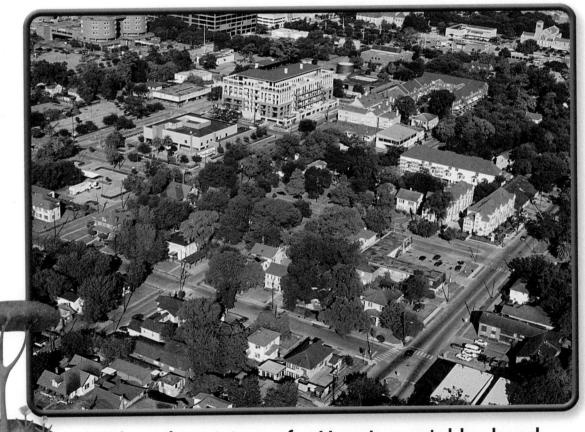

**Look at this picture of a Houston neighborhood taken from above.**

**This is a map of the same neighborhood.**

GEOGRAPHY THEME How are places shown on this map?

**LESSON 1**
**Review**

① **Vocabulary** What is a **neighborhood**?

② How are a picture and a map the same? How are they different?

③ List some places that people share in your neighborhood.

# Use a Map Key

**Vocabulary**

**map key**

| | |
|---|---|
|  | Children's Museum |
|  | Community Center |
|  | Golf Course |
|  | Houston Museum of Natural Science |
|  | Japanese Garden |
|  | Rice University |
|  | Zoo |

**Map Key**

| | |
|---|---|
| | Street |

▶ **Why It Matters**

Symbols help you find places on a map.

▶ **What You Need to Know**

A **map key** lists the symbols used on a map. It shows you what they mean.

▶ **Practice the Skill**

❶ What is the symbol for the zoo?

❷ Find the Community Center. On what street is it located?

❸ What is near the lake?

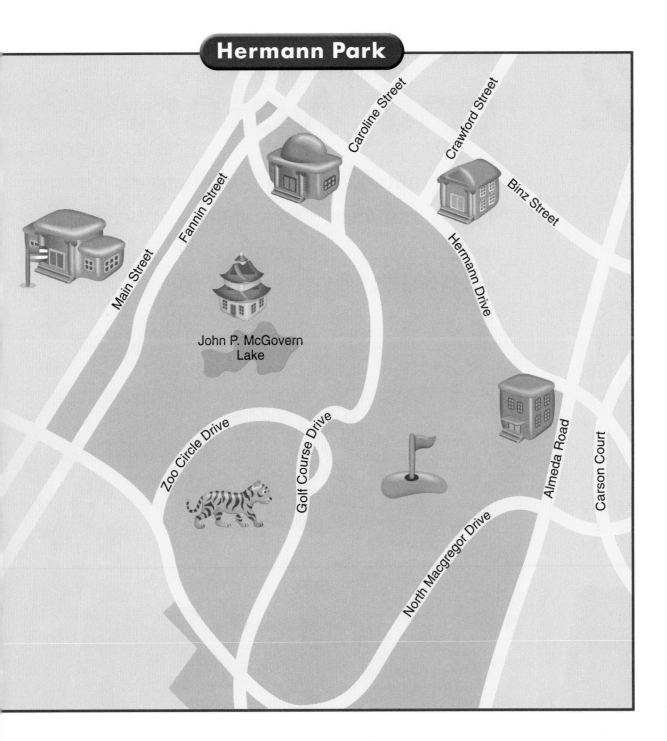

Hermann Park

Caroline Street
Crawford Street
Binz Street
Fannin Street
Main Street
Hermann Drive
John P. McGovern Lake
Zoo Circle Drive
Golf Course Drive
Almeda Road
Carson Court
North Macgregor Drive

## ▶ Apply What You Learned

Make a map of your community.

Use symbols and a map key.

Practice your map and globe skills
with the **GeoSkills CD-ROM.**

# Land and Water

**Main Idea**
There are many kinds of land and water.

**Vocabulary**

valley

mountain

lake

hill

plain

island

river

Communities can be in many places. This community is in a **valley** between mountains. A **mountain** is the highest kind of land.

Sawtooth Mountains

Dear Aunt Patty,

I'm having a great time in Sun Valley!

Love,
Tony

Visit Sun Valley, Idaho

This community is near a lake. There is land all around the water of a **lake**. Lakes can be large or small, shallow or deep.

California
USA

Sun Valley
Aug '04, 2003
Idaho, USA

California Quail & California Poppy

Patty Hosley
234 Sea Dr.
Orlando, FL 12345

Silver Lake,
Massachusetts

There are other kinds of land. A **hill** is land that rises above the land around it. Hills are not as high as mountains.

The Hills of **California**

A **plain** is land that is mostly flat. The land in most plains is good for growing food.

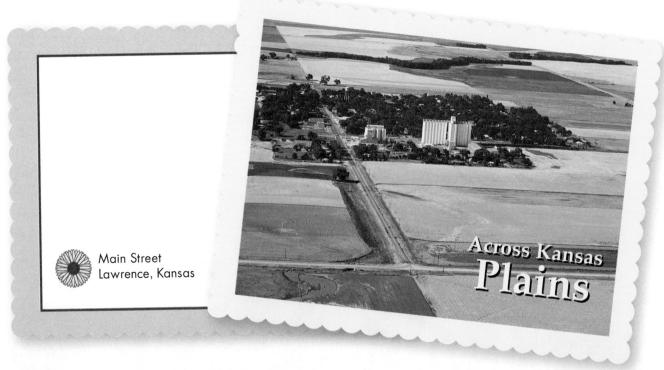

Main Street
Lawrence, Kansas

Across Kansas **Plains**

An **island** is land that has water all around it.

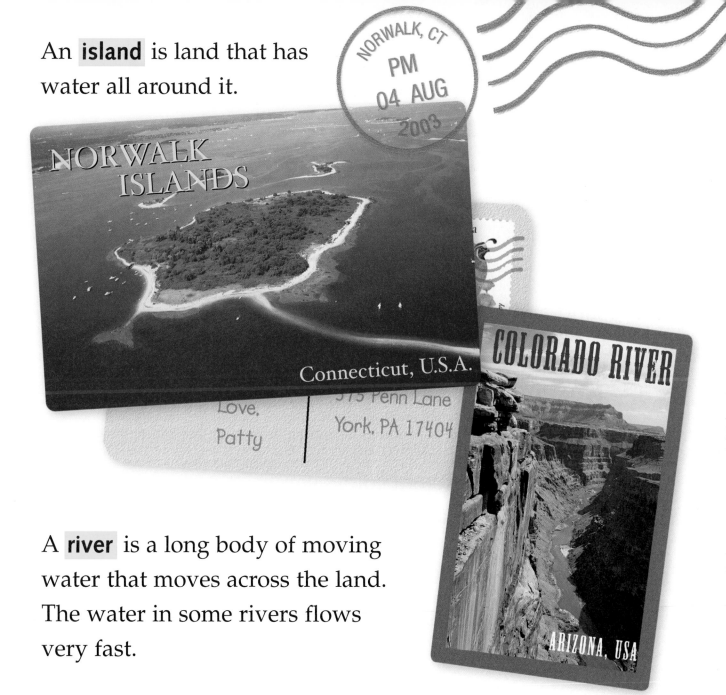

NORWALK ISLANDS

Connecticut, U.S.A.

NORWALK, CT
PM
04 AUG
2003

Love,
Patty

575 Penn Lane
York, PA 17404

COLORADO RIVER

ARIZONA, USA

A **river** is a long body of moving water that moves across the land. The water in some rivers flows very fast.

LESSON 2
Review

1. **Vocabulary** What is the difference between a **mountain** and a **plain**?

2. What kinds of land and water are near your community?

3. Choose a kind of land and a kind of water. Draw a picture of each.

# Find Land and Water on a Map

## ▶ Why It Matters

Seeing land and water on maps can help you imagine what places look like.

## ▶ What You Need to Know

Texas is a large state. It has many kinds of land and water. Different colors show the different kinds of land and water.

## ▶ Practice the Skill

**1** Describe the symbols for land and water on the map.

**2** Name two rivers in Texas.

**3** Which city is found in the mountains?

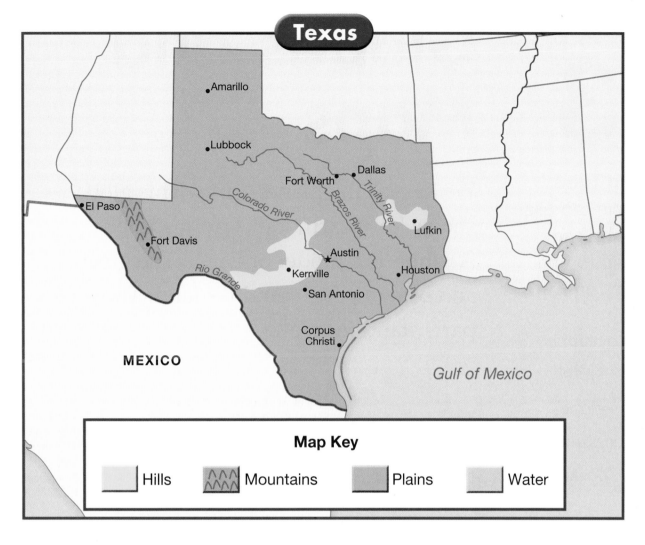

Texas

**Map Key**

Hills | Mountains | Plains | Water

## Apply What You Learned

Look at a map of your state. Find the different kinds of land and water.

Practice your map and globe skills with the **GeoSkills CD-ROM**.

# Globes and Maps

**Main Idea**
People can use a globe and a map to find places on Earth.

**Vocabulary**

Earth

globe

continent

ocean

We live on the planet **Earth**. This globe shows how Earth looks from space. A **globe** is a model of Earth. The green and brown parts stand for land. The blue parts stand for water.

Like a globe, a map can also show all the places on Earth. The seven large areas of land are **continents**. We live on the continent of North America. Between most of the continents are oceans. An **ocean** is a very large body of salty water.

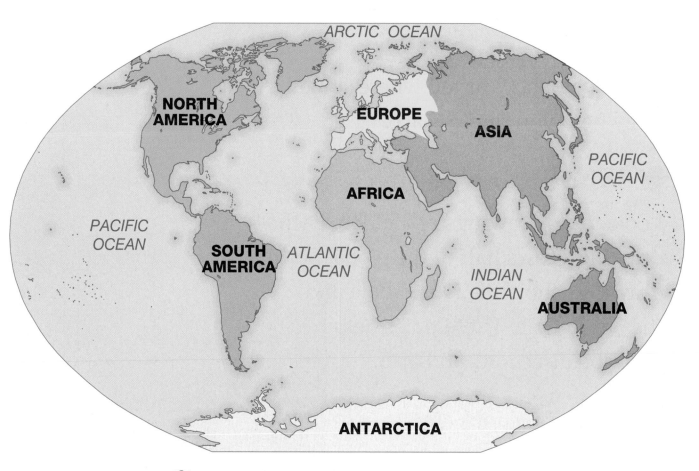

ARCTIC OCEAN

NORTH AMERICA

EUROPE

ASIA

PACIFIC OCEAN

AFRICA

PACIFIC OCEAN

SOUTH AMERICA

ATLANTIC OCEAN

INDIAN OCEAN

AUSTRALIA

ANTARCTICA

GEOGRAPHY THEME

Which oceans are near North America?

**LESSON 3**
**Review**

❶ **Vocabulary** How is a map like a **globe**?

❷ Name two oceans.

❸ Locate the United States on a globe.

# Find Directions on a Globe

## ▶ Why It Matters

**Directions** show or tell where something is. They help you find a place.

## ▶ What You Need to Know

Look at the drawings of a globe. Each drawing shows half of the globe. Both drawings show the North Pole and the South Pole. These poles help describe directions on Earth.

The main directions are north, south, east, and west. North is the direction toward the North Pole. When you face north, east is to your right. West is to your left.

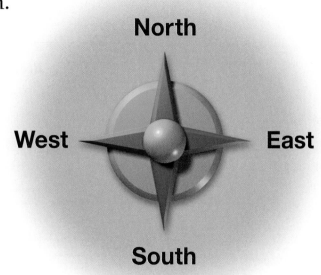

North

West            East

South

# ▶ Practice the Skill

**①** Which continent is east of Europe?

**②** Which continent is at the South Pole?

**③** Which ocean is west of North America?

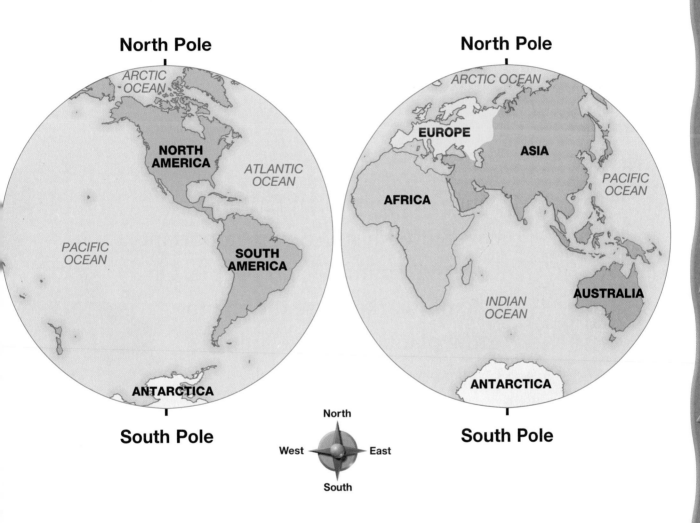

North Pole

ARCTIC OCEAN

NORTH AMERICA

ATLANTIC OCEAN

PACIFIC OCEAN

SOUTH AMERICA

ANTARCTICA

South Pole

North Pole

ARCTIC OCEAN

EUROPE

ASIA

PACIFIC OCEAN

AFRICA

AUSTRALIA

INDIAN OCEAN

ANTARCTICA

South Pole

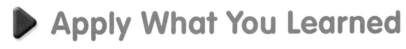

North

West — East

South

# ▶ Apply What You Learned

Make a model of Earth.

Practice your map and globe skills
with the **GeoSkills CD-ROM**.

# People and Resources

**Main Idea**
Natural resources are important to people.

How are paper, bread, and gasoline alike? They are all made from Earth's resources. A **resource** is anything people can use. Earth has many resources.

## Soil

Much of the land on Earth is covered with soil. Soil is important to plants, animals, and people. On a **farm**, workers use the soil to grow plants and raise animals that people use for food.

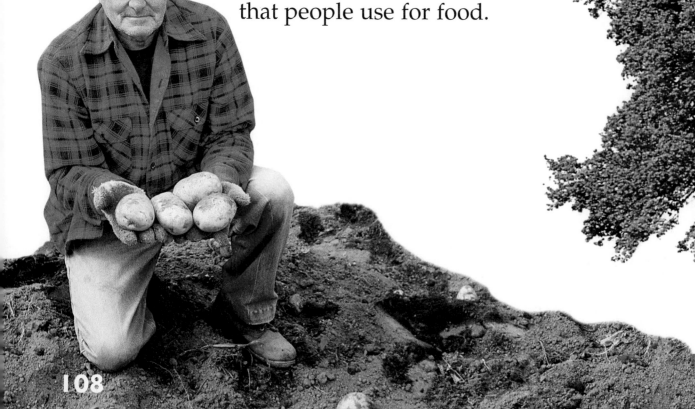

# Trees

A **forest** is a large area where many trees grow. Wood from trees is used to make furniture and buildings. Some trees give us food, such as apples and walnuts.

# Oil and Gas

Oil and gas come from under the ground. People use oil and gas to heat their homes and cook their food. Some oil is made into gasoline for running cars and other machines.

## A CLOSER LOOK
### Drilling for Oil

People drill holes deep into the ground to reach oil. An engine turns the drill pipe so that it cuts down through rock in the ground. When the drill reaches oil, the oil is pumped up through the pipe. **How do people reach the oil under the ground?**

derrick

engine house

drill pipe

rock

oil

# Water

Water is a resource that all living things must have to live. People and animals drink it, and some plants and animals live in it.

**LESSON 4 Review**

1. **Vocabulary** How do **resources** help you?

2. What natural resources are in or near your community?

3. Make a list of ways people use water.

# Predict What Will Happen

**Vocabulary**

predict

weather

## ▶ Why It Matters

When you know how things happen, you can **predict**, or tell ahead of time, what will happen next. Knowing what is going to happen can help people plan what to do.

## ▶ What You Need to Know

People can predict the weather by looking at clouds. **Weather** is what the air outside is like. Dark clouds often mean rain is coming.

## ▶ Practice the Skill

**1** If it did not rain for a long time, what would happen to growing food?

**2** Think about the people who make, sell, and buy food. Tell what you think would happen to them.

## ▶ Apply What You Learned

What do you think would happen if people caught all the fish they could find?

# Saving Our Resources

**Main Idea**
People need to take care of Earth's natural resources.

**Vocabulary**
pollution
litter
recycle

Many people live on Earth. They all use the same resources.

## Protect Our Resources

It is important to keep earth and our resources clean. **Pollution** is anything that makes air, land, or water dirty.

Laws help. You can help, too. Do not **litter**, or throw trash, on land or in water.

### Marjory Stoneman Douglas
**1890–1998**
**Character Trait: Responsibility**

Marjory Stoneman Douglas loved the Everglades, the low, wet grasslands in southern Florida. Thanks to her help, laws now protect the Everglades and its wildlife.

MULTIMEDIA BIOGRAPHIES
Visit The Learning Site at
www.harcourtschool.com/biographies
to learn about other famous people.

**GO** ONLINE

# Use Resources Wisely

You can reduce, or use less of a resource.

You can reuse, or use some things over and over again.

You can recycle, or make something old into something new.

Recycle

**LESSON 5**
**Review**

❶ **Vocabulary**   Why is it important not to **litter**?

❷ Why should people use less of a resource?

❸ Make a poster showing how you can use resources wisely at home.

# Houses and Homes

**Main Idea**
People around the world live in all kinds of homes.

Vocabulary

desert

People around the world have different kinds of homes. Some live in houses. Others live in buildings with many apartments.

**Germany**

**Canada**

**Brazil**

People build homes using the resources of the land where they live. These homes in Congo have roofs made from straw, or dried grass.

**Congo**

**Mexico**

People also have to think about the weather where they build their homes. This place in Mexico is built of clay bricks dried in the hot desert sun. A **desert** is land that gets little rain.

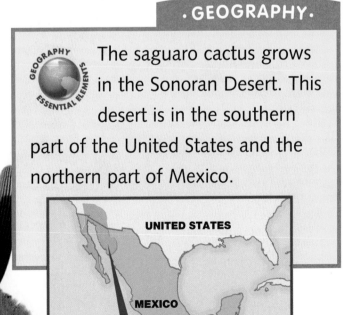

**.GEOGRAPHY.**

GEOGRAPHY ESSENTIAL ELEMENTS

The saguaro cactus grows in the Sonoran Desert. This desert is in the southern part of the United States and the northern part of Mexico.

UNITED STATES

MEXICO

**Sonoran Desert**

This house is in Norway. It is made from the trees in the forest around it.

**Norway**

When it rains a lot, this river in the Amazon rain forest can flood. This house in Venezuela is built on stilts. They keep it dry above the river's water.

**Venezuela**

Some places are crowded. These homes in Italy are built close together. There is little open space between the homes.

**Italy**

**China**

This city in China has very little land for new homes. Some people live on boats.

**LESSON 6**
**Review**

① **Vocabulary**   How is a **desert** different from a forest?

② Why do people have to think about the weather when they build their homes?

③ Describe the types of houses in your neighborhood.

# A Butterfly Garden

## Get Ready

Planting a flower garden makes any place more beautiful. Some flowers are favorites of butterflies. These students decided to plant a butterfly garden outside their school.

## What to See

Each student draws a plan for the new butterfly garden.

**Then**

Butterfly gardens need to get lots of sun but not much wind.

The students work in the garden to care for the flowers.

**Now**

Students celebrate the new garden with a party.

## Take a Field Trip

**GO ONLINE**

**A VIRTUAL TOUR**
Visit The Learning Site at **www.harcourtschool.com/tours** to take virtual tours of other parks and scenic areas.

**A VIDEO TOUR**

READING RAINBOW

Check your media center or classroom library for a video featuring a segment from Reading Rainbow.

# Review and Test Preparation

## Visual Summary

Complete this web. Write or draw to show what you learned in this unit.

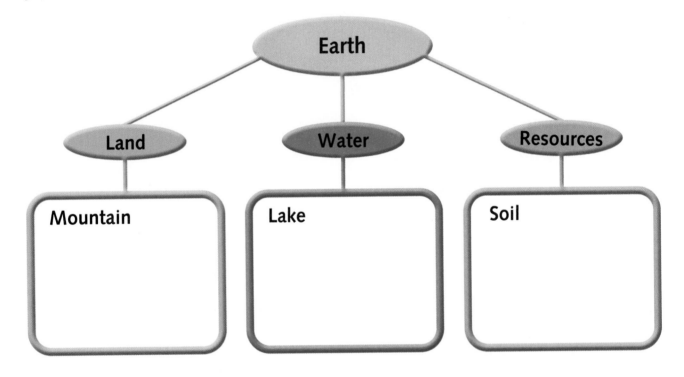

Earth

Land

Water

Resources

Mountain

Lake

Soil

## THINK & WRITE

**Look at Pictures** Look at homes in books and magazines. Look for clues that show what the weather is like there.

**Write a Caption** Choose one of the homes. Write a sentence telling about the weather in that picture.

Draw a picture to show the meaning of each word.

**1** neighborhood

(p. 94)

**3** resource

(p. 108)

**2** ocean

(p. 105)

**4** weather

(p. 112)

## Recall Facts

**5** How many continents are there?

**6** How are a river and an ocean different?

**7** Name two kinds of resources.

**8** How do farmers use soil?

**9** On which continent do you live?

**A** Africa

**C** North America

**B** Australia

**D** South America

**10** Which resource do people use to build homes?

**F** water

**H** oil

**G** soil

**J** trees

⓫ How can being able to predict what will happen help people plan what to do?

⓬ Why is it important to take care of Earth's resources?

**Apply Map and Globe Skills**

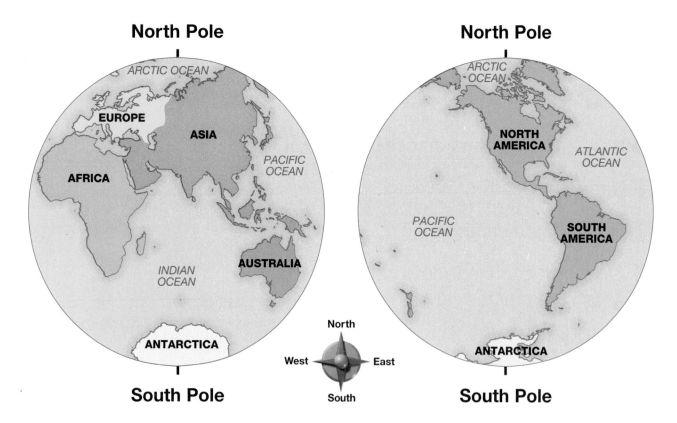

⓭ If you traveled south from North America, on what continent would you be?

⓮ Which ocean is west of Australia?

⓯ Is Antarctica north or south of Africa?

⓰ Which ocean is at the North Pole?

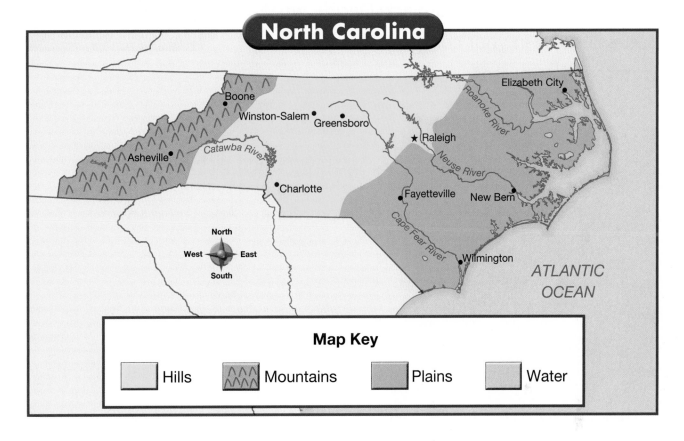

**North Carolina**

Elizabeth City

Boone
Winston-Salem Greensboro
Roanoke River
★ Raleigh
Asheville
Catawba River
Neuse River
Charlotte
Fayetteville New Bern
North
West — East
South
Cape Fear River
Wilmington
ATLANTIC
OCEAN

**Map Key**

Hills ∧∧∧ Mountains Plains Water

**17** Name the ocean that is east of North Carolina.

**18** What kind of land is around Boone?

**19** What kind of land is in the middle of the state?

**20** Name a city that is on the plains.

# Unit Activities

**Complete the Unit Project** Work with your group to finish the unit project. Decide what you will show in your collage about land, water, and resources.

**GO** ONLINE

Visit The Learning Site at www.harcourtschool.com/ socialstudies/activities for additional activities.

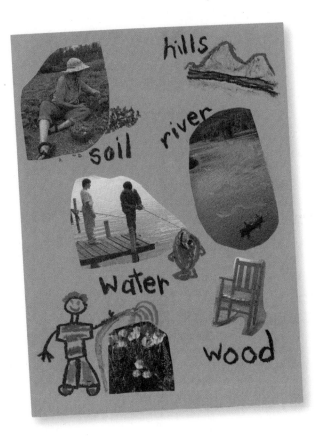

## Land and Water

Draw or find pictures that show the land and water around your community. Add these to your collage.

## Using Resources

Draw or find pictures that show how people use these resources.

- soil
- trees
- oil and gas
- water

## Visit Your Library

**Compost! Growing Gardens from Your Garbage** by Linda Glaser. Find out how a family recycles food leftovers.

**Me on the Map** by Joan Sweeney. A young girl shows where she is in the world.

**Haystack** by Bonnie and Arthur Geisert. See how important a haystack is on a farm.

# All About People

· Mexican maracas ·

# All About People

**"** We all sing with the same voice. **"**

—J. Phillip Miller, Sheppard McGreene, *Sesame Street*, 1983

## Preview the Content

As you read, look for facts about culture. Write down the facts you find. After you read, write a sentence that tells the big idea of this unit.

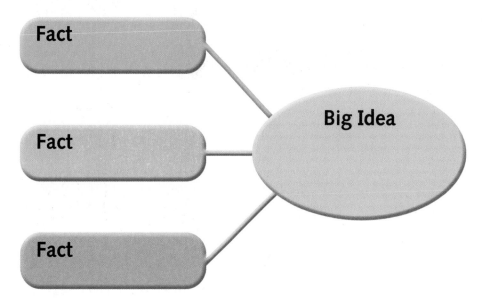

Fact

Fact

Fact

Big Idea

**role** The part a person plays in a group or community. (page 134)

**needs** Things people must have to live. (page 138)

130

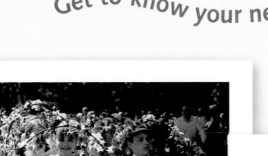

**culture** A group's way of life. (page 143)

**celebration** A time to be happy about something special. (page 154)

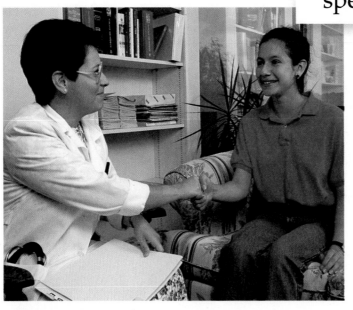

**custom** A group's way of doing something. (page 160)

**131**

# The Mohawk Way

## from *Time for Kids*

Kids at the Akwesasne (AH•kwe•zah•sneh) Freedom School in Rooseveltown, New York, don't speak English in class. They speak Mohawk, the **language** of their Native American ancestors. Children from kindergarten to sixth grade learn all their subjects in Mohawk. Learning about their own people makes the kids feel proud!

Kids enjoy Mohawk music and dancing.

132

Even art projects help kids learn about their tribe. This girl is building a paper longhouse.

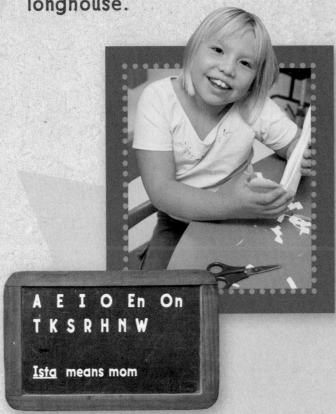

A E I O En On
T K S R H N W

Ista means mom

## How many?

The Mohawk language has 13 letters. English has 26 letters—twice as many.

# Think About It

1 Why do the children at this school learn in a different language?

2 Find out about the Native Americans in your state.

## Read a Book

## Start the Unit Project

**A World Culture Book** Your class will make a book to show some of the cultures in our world. As you read this unit, think about how people are the same and different.

## Use Technology

Visit The Learning Site at **www.harcourtschool.com/ socialstudies** for additional activities, primary sources, and other resources to use in this unit.

# People Together

I belong to many groups. I am a member of my family, my class, my school, and more.

Each person in a group has a role. A **role** is the part that a person plays in a group he or she belongs to.

I am.

I am a daughter.
I set the table for dinner.

I am a first grader.
I water our class plants.

I am a soccer goalie.
I keep the other team
from scoring.

I am in an art club. I make
sure there are enough
brushes for everyone.

**LESSON 1**
**Review**

1 **Vocabulary** What are your **roles** in school?

2 How do you depend on other people in your groups?

3 Think about the groups you belong to. Make a chart to show your role in each group.

# Skills

**CITIZENSHIP**

# Solve a Problem

Vocabulary

problem

solution

▶ **Why It Matters**

Sometimes people have problems. A **problem** is something that is hard to understand or to do. A problem needs a **solution**, or answer. You can work in a group to solve a problem.

▶ **What You Need to Know**

Follow these steps when you need to solve a problem.

**Step 1** Name the problem.

**Step 2** Think of some solutions.

**Step 3** Talk about the solutions. Choose the best one.

**Step 4** Follow your plan to solve the problem.

**Step 5** Talk about how well the problem was solved.

**136**

## ▶ Practice the Skill

There are two computers in the classroom, and four children need to use them. Work in a group to solve this problem. Use the steps on page 136.

## ▶ Apply What You Learned

What would you do if you lost something you had borrowed? Write about how you would use the steps to solve the problem.

# Families Together

**Main Idea**
People have needs that they meet in different ways.

**Vocabulary**

needs

shelter

All people have needs. **Needs** are things we must have to live. We must have food, clothing, and **shelter**, or a place to live in. Family members help take care of each other's needs.

food

clothing

shelter

**food**

Families all over the world have the same needs. Some meet their needs in the same ways your family does. Some meet their needs in different ways.

**clothing**

shelter

**FAST FACT** Imagine having grass for a roof! Thatched roofs are made from tall grasses called reeds. A layer of reeds 12 inches thick makes the roof waterproof.

1 **Vocabulary** What **needs** do people have?

2 Describe ways your family meets its needs.

3 Draw a picture showing how your family meets its needs for food, clothing, and shelter.

# What Is Culture?

**Main Idea**
People around the world have different cultures.

**Vocabulary**

culture

religion

My aunt Shelly loves to travel. She has met people who have different cultures.

They have great food in Denmark!

A **culture** is a group's way of life. I learned about cultures by helping my Aunt Shelly make this scrapbook.

Dolls from Peru

People sometimes wear kimonos in Japan.

This Inuit girl in Canada plays string games.

People in different culture groups
have different **religions**, or beliefs.

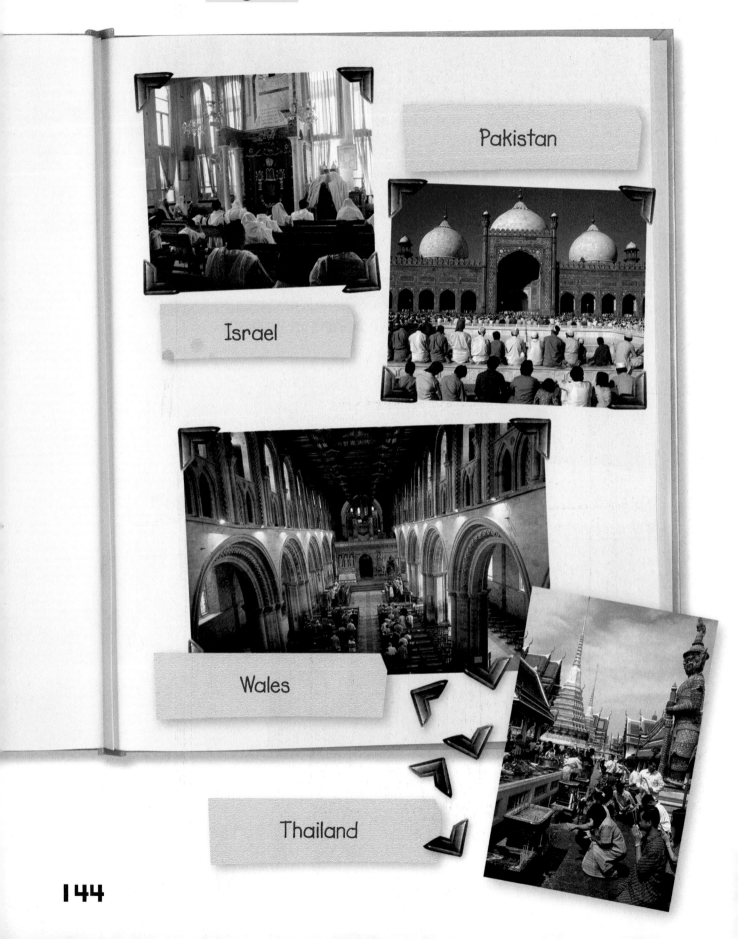

Pakistan

Israel

Wales

Thailand

144

Aunt Shelly learned how to say some things in different languages. <u>Friend</u> is one of her favorite words. <u>Tomodachi</u> means "friend" in Japanese.

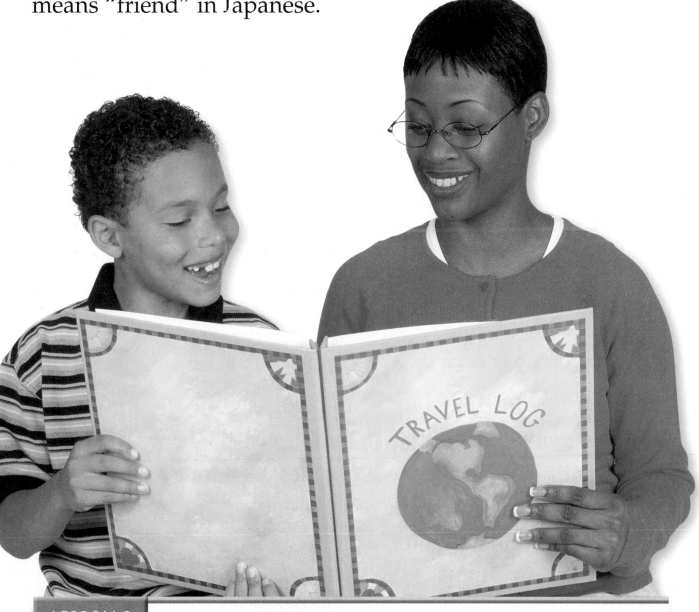

**LESSON 3**
**Review**

1 **Vocabulary**   What kinds of things are part of a group's **culture**?

2 Why is language important?

3 Cut out magazine pictures to make a poster about culture.

# Point of View

| Vocabulary |
| --- |
| point of view |

## ▶ Why It Matters

What is your favorite color? What is your friend's favorite color? You may think red is the best color. Your friend may think blue is. Not everyone thinks the same way. What you think is your **point of view**.

## ▶ What You Need to Know

Everyone needs to eat, but people like different kinds of food. Italian families eat many kinds of pasta. Chinese families eat a lot of rice. Different cultures have different points of view about foods.

# ▶ Practice the Skill

**①** Look at the pictures of different breakfast foods. Which would you choose? Why?

**②** Which is better, a hot breakfast or a cold breakfast? Why do you think so?

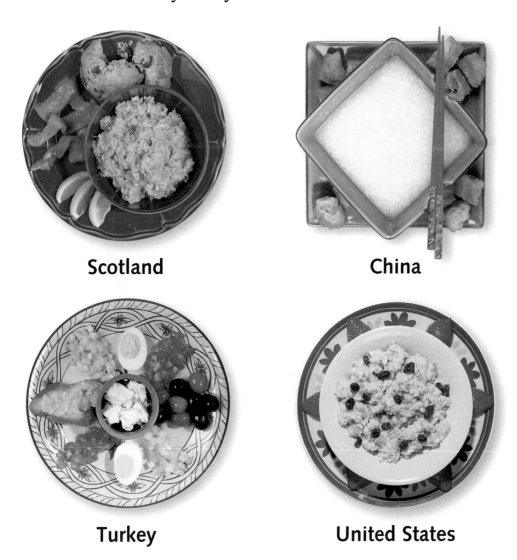

Scotland

China

Turkey

United States

# ▶ Apply What You Learned

Talk with your classmates about the foods you like best for lunch.

# Expressing Culture

The foods people eat, the clothes they wear, and the languages they speak all show their culture. Music, dance, and other arts are also part of culture.

What do these pictures show about cultures?

Kente cloth from Ghana

Dancer from Thailand

Sitar from India

Mask from Greece

Bark painting from Australia

Pomo basket from California

Stories are part of every culture. A **fable** is a made-up story that teaches a lesson. "The Hare and the Tortoise" is a fable that is still told today.

The Fables of Æsop

Selected, and their History traced, by Joseph Jacobs

Illustrated by Richard Heighway

1894 book

# The Hare and the Tortoise

### a fable by Aesop

Hare always boasted that he was the fastest animal. He made fun of Tortoise because she moved so slowly. One day Tortoise said, "If we raced, I might beat you. Let's race to the main road and see who wins."

Hare laughed, but he agreed to race. He started off at top speed and soon left Tortoise far behind. Hare was so sure he would win that he decided to take a nap.

Tortoise did not stop. She just kept going slow and steady. When Hare woke up, he saw that he had been wrong. Tortoise had won the race.

**Lesson** The fastest one doesn't always get there first. Slow and steady wins the race.

Story cloth from Vietnam

Puppet from Indonesia

## Activity

Make paper puppets of Tortoise and Hare.
Then use them to retell the story.

## Research

Visit The Learning Site at
**www.harcourtschool.com/primarysources**
to research other primary sources.

# Skills

MAP AND GLOBE

# Use a Map Scale

**Vocabulary**

distance

map scale

## ▶ Why It Matters

A map shows a place smaller than it really is, but it can show real distance. **Distance** is how far one place is from another.

## ▶ What You Need to Know

A map scale helps you find out how far apart places are. A **map scale**, like a ruler, is used to measure distance.

## ▶ Practice the Skill

1 Lay a strip of paper so its edge touches the • in the Basket Room and the • in the Restaurant. Mark where each • is.

2 Place the paper along the map scale. One of the marks must be at zero.

3 How many yards are there between the two rooms?

**152**

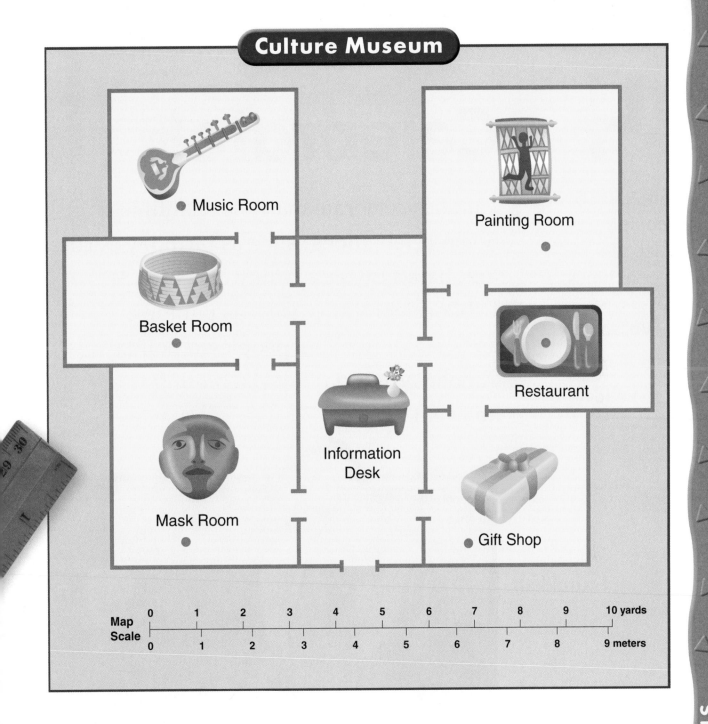

**Culture Museum**

Music Room

Painting Room

Basket Room

Restaurant

Mask Room

Information Desk

Gift Shop

| Map Scale | 0 | 1 | 2 | 3 | 4 | 5 | 6 | 7 | 8 | 9 | 10 yards |
| | 0 | 1 | 2 | 3 | 4 | 5 | 6 | 7 | 8 | | 9 meters |

## ▶ Apply What You Learned

Make a map of your classroom. Show a map scale and symbols.

Practice your map and globe skills with the **GeoSkills CD-ROM.**

# 4

## Celebrate!

**Main Idea**
People celebrate special times.

**Vocabulary**
celebration
holiday

Families celebrate many special times. Some **celebrations**, such as birthday parties, are shared by only family and friends. Other celebrations, such as parades, are shared by many people on holidays. A **holiday** is a day for celebrating an event.

Hanukkah

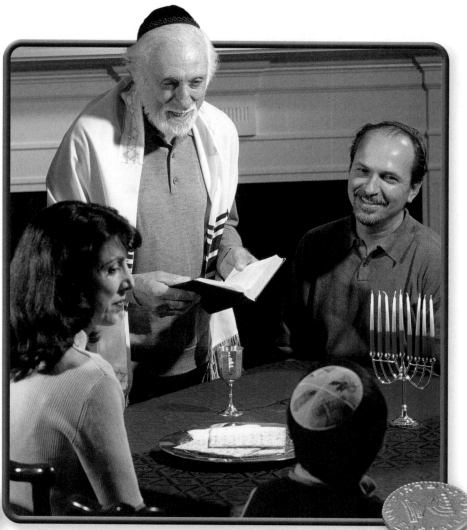

On some holidays, people celebrate something in their religion. Families have special meals and activities on these days.

Christmas

Three Kings Day

Some celebrations come from other countries. When people move to the United States, they still celebrate the holidays they love. This helps them remember where they came from. Their celebrations show their culture.

**Chinese New Year**

**Cinco de Mayo**

### Kwanzaa

Kwanzaa is a week-long holiday when African American families celebrate their culture. This holiday is new, but the ideas for it come from very old African beliefs. During Kwanzaa, families remember what is important to them.

**Cherry Blossom Festival**

**Highland Games**

All people are special.

**LESSON 4**
**Review**

1. **Vocabulary** How do **celebrations** teach us about other countries?

2. What are some things your family does to celebrate special times?

3. Make a greeting card for a holiday or a celebration.

# Use a Calendar

**Vocabulary**

calendar

▶ ## Why It Matters

A **calendar** is used to measure time.

▶ ## What You Need to Know

A calendar shows days, weeks, and months.
A week has 7 days. A year has 365 days in 52
weeks. There are also 12 months in a year.

| January | | | | | | |
|---|---|---|---|---|---|---|
| S | M | T | W | Th | F | S |
| | | | 1 | 2 | 3 | 4 |
| 5 | 6 | 7 | 8 | 9 | 10 | 11 |
| 12 | 13 | 14 | 15 | 16 | 17 | 18 |
| 19 | 20 | 21 | 22 | 23 | 24 | 25 |
| 26 | 27 | 28 | 29 | 30 | 31 | |

| February | | | | | | |
|---|---|---|---|---|---|---|
| S | M | T | W | Th | F | S |
| | | | | | | 1 |
| 2 | 3 | 4 | 5 | 6 | 7 | 8 |
| 9 | 10 | 11 | 12 | 13 | 14 | 15 |
| 16 | 17 | 18 | 19 | 20 | 21 | 22 |
| 23 | 24 | 25 | 26 | 27 | 28 | |

| March | | | | | | |
|---|---|---|---|---|---|---|
| S | M | T | W | Th | F | S |
| | | | | | | 1 |
| 2 | 3 | 4 | 5 | 6 | 7 | 8 |
| 9 | 10 | 11 | 12 | 13 | 14 | 15 |
| 16 | 17 | 18 | 19 | 20 | 21 | 22 |
| 23 | 24 | 25 | 26 | 27 | 28 | 29 |
| 30 | 31 | | | | | |

| April | | | | | | |
|---|---|---|---|---|---|---|
| S | M | T | W | Th | F | S |
| | | 1 | 2 | 3 | 4 | 5 |
| 6 | 7 | 8 | 9 | 10 | 11 | 12 |
| 13 | 14 | 15 | 16 | 17 | 18 | 19 |
| 20 | 21 | 22 | 23 | 24 | 25 | 26 |
| 27 | 28 | 29 | 30 | | | |

| May | | | | | | |
|---|---|---|---|---|---|---|
| S | M | T | W | Th | F | S |
| | | | | 1 | 2 | 3 |
| 4 | 5 | 6 | 7 | 8 | 9 | 10 |
| 11 | 12 | 13 | 14 | 15 | 16 | 17 |
| 18 | 19 | 20 | 21 | 22 | 23 | 24 |
| 25 | 26 | 27 | 28 | 29 | 30 | 31 |

| June | | | | | | |
|---|---|---|---|---|---|---|
| S | M | T | W | Th | F | S |
| 1 | 2 | 3 | 4 | 5 | 6 | 7 |
| 8 | 9 | 10 | 11 | 12 | 13 | 14 |
| 15 | 16 | 17 | 18 | 19 | 20 | 21 |
| 22 | 23 | 24 | 25 | 26 | 27 | 28 |
| 29 | 30 | | | | | |

| July | | | | | | |
|---|---|---|---|---|---|---|
| S | M | T | W | Th | F | S |
| | | 1 | 2 | 3 | 4 | 5 |
| 6 | 7 | 8 | 9 | 10 | 11 | 12 |
| 13 | 14 | 15 | 16 | 17 | 18 | 19 |
| 20 | 21 | 22 | 23 | 24 | 25 | 26 |
| 27 | 28 | 29 | 30 | 31 | | |

| August | | | | | | |
|---|---|---|---|---|---|---|
| S | M | T | W | Th | F | S |
| | | | | | 1 | 2 |
| 3 | 4 | 5 | 6 | 7 | 8 | 9 |
| 10 | 11 | 12 | 13 | 14 | 15 | 16 |
| 17 | 18 | 19 | 20 | 21 | 22 | 23 |
| 24 | 25 | 26 | 27 | 28 | 29 | 30 |
| 31 | | | | | | |

| September | | | | | | |
|---|---|---|---|---|---|---|
| S | M | T | W | Th | F | S |
| | 1 | 2 | 3 | 4 | 5 | 6 |
| 7 | 8 | 9 | 10 | 11 | 12 | 13 |
| 14 | 15 | 16 | 17 | 18 | 19 | 20 |
| 21 | 22 | 23 | 24 | 25 | 26 | 27 |
| 28 | 29 | 30 | | | | |

| October | | | | | | |
|---|---|---|---|---|---|---|
| S | M | T | W | Th | F | S |
| | | | 1 | 2 | 3 | 4 |
| 5 | 6 | 7 | 8 | 9 | 10 | 11 |
| 12 | 13 | 14 | 15 | 16 | 17 | 18 |
| 19 | 20 | 21 | 22 | 23 | 24 | 25 |
| 26 | 27 | 28 | 29 | 30 | 31 | |

| November | | | | | | |
|---|---|---|---|---|---|---|
| S | M | T | W | Th | F | S |
| | | | | | | 1 |
| 2 | 3 | 4 | 5 | 6 | 7 | 8 |
| 9 | 10 | 11 | 12 | 13 | 14 | 15 |
| 16 | 17 | 18 | 19 | 20 | 21 | 22 |
| 23 | 24 | 25 | 26 | 27 | 28 | 29 |
| 30 | | | | | | |

| December | | | | | | |
|---|---|---|---|---|---|---|
| S | M | T | W | Th | F | S |
| | 1 | 2 | 3 | 4 | 5 | 6 |
| 7 | 8 | 9 | 10 | 11 | 12 | 13 |
| 14 | 15 | 16 | 17 | 18 | 19 | 20 |
| 21 | 22 | 23 | 24 | 25 | 26 | 27 |
| 28 | 29 | 30 | 31 | | | |

## Practice the Skill

1. Look at the calendar. How many days are in December?

2. Which comes first, Christmas or Hanukkah?

3. When is New Year's Eve?

# December

| Sunday | Monday | Tuesday | Wednesday | Thursday | Friday | Saturday |
|---|---|---|---|---|---|---|
| | 1 | 2 | 3 | 4 | 5 | 6 St. Nicholas Day |
| 7 | 8 | 9 | 10 | 11 | 12 | 13 Santa Lucia |
| 14 | 15 | 16 Las Posadas | 17 | 18 | 19 Hanukkah | 20 |
| 21 | 22 First Day of Winter | 23 | 24 | 25 Christmas | 26 Kwanzaa | 27 |
| 28 | 29 | 30 | 31 New Year's Eve | | | |

## Apply What You Learned

Make a calendar for the month of your birthday. Find out what other special days are in that month. Mark those days on your calendar.

# We Are Americans!

**Main Idea**
Americans share many customs.

**Vocabulary**
custom

Our families have come from around the world to live in the United States. We share American **customs**, or ways of doing things. We also share customs from other countries. We are all Americans.

1 **Vocabulary** What is a **custom**?

2 Think about a custom your family has. Why is it important?

3 Work with a partner to list customs you see in your community.

# A Festival of ·Cultures·

## Get Ready

Americans come from many countries and cultures. Visitors to a festival can learn about the customs of other cultures. They can enjoy special dances, music, food, clothing, and crafts.

## What to See

At this festival, people wear clothing that shows their different cultures.

Music is an important part of Mexican culture.

A Swedish woman makes a doll out of corn husks.

A man cooks plantains, which are like bananas. Plantains are a common food in Nigeria.

A Japanese woman dances with fans. Fans have been used in Japan for more than a thousand years.

## Take a Field Trip

**GO** ONLINE

**A VIRTUAL TOUR**
Visit The Learning Site at
**www.harcourtschool.com/tours**
to take virtual tours of
other cultures.

READING RAINBOW

**A VIDEO TOUR**
Check your media
center or classroom library
for a video featuring a segment
from Reading Rainbow.

## Visual Summary

Finish the chart. In the rectangle, write one more fact you learned. In the oval, write the big idea of this unit.

**Fact** Some people in Japan wear kimonos.

**Fact** People speak different languages.

**Fact**

**Big Idea**

## THINK & WRITE

**Make a Note** Think about how your family and families you know meet their needs. Make a note of the different ways.

**Write a Paragraph** Describe similarities and differences in ways families meet each need.

Write the word that completes each sentence.

**1** My _____ at home is to be a helper.

**2** Shaking hands is an American _____ .

**3** Food, clothing, and shelter are all _____ .

**4** A birthday party is a kind of _____ .

**5** A group's _____ shows in its music, dance, and other arts.

role
(p. 134)

needs
(p. 138)

culture
(p. 143)

celebration
(p. 154)

custom
(p. 160)

## Recall Facts

**6** What are some ways people share their culture?

**7** What does a map scale measure?

**8** How are all Americans the same?

**9** Which of these is a week-long African American holiday?

**A** Highland Games

**B** Kwanzaa

**C** Cherry Blossom Festival

**D** Chinese New Year

**10** Which of these is the number of months in the year?

**F** 7

**G** 52

**H** 12

**J** 365

**11** Three children want to play a game that only two can play. How would you solve this problem?

**12** Why do you think people celebrate holidays from other countries?

**Apply Chart and Graph Skills**

## October

| Sunday | Monday | Tuesday | Wednesday | Thursday | Friday | Saturday |
|--------|--------|---------|-----------|----------|--------|----------|
| | | | 1 Open House | 2 | 3 | 4 |
| 5 | 6 | 7 | 8 | 9 | 10 | 11 Eleanor Roosevelt's Birthday |
| 12 | 13 Columbus Day | 14 | 15 | 16  Dictionary Day | 17 | 18 |
| 19 | 20 | 21 | 22 | 23 | 24 | 25 |
| 26 | 27 Picture Day | 28 | 29 | 30 | 31 Harvest Festival | |

**13** How many days are in this month?

**14** When is Dictionary Day?

**15** What happens on October 27?

**16** On which day of the week is the Harvest Festival?

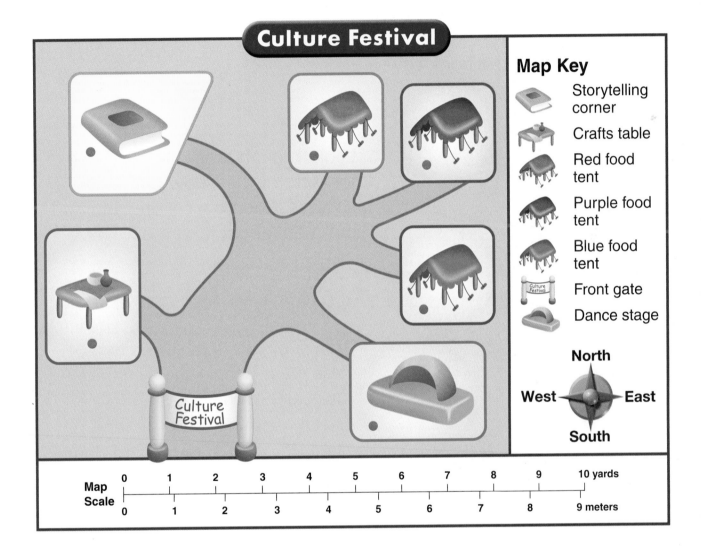

17 How many yards is it from the storytelling corner to the crafts table?

18 How far is it from the purple food tent to the blue food tent?

19 From the front gate, in which direction is the dance stage?

20 What is south of the blue food tent?

# Unit Activities

**Complete the Unit Project** Work with your group to finish the unit project. Decide how you will show people and their cultures in your book. Make the book cover.

**GO ONLINE**

Visit The Learning Site at www.harcourtschool.com/socialstudies/activities for additional activities.

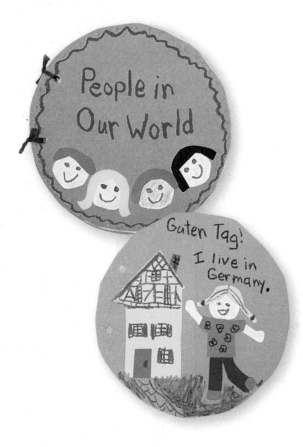

People in Our World

Guten Tag! I live in Germany.

## Find Out

Look through magazines and books for pictures that show different cultures. Choose a culture, and find out more about it.

## Share a Culture

Draw a picture that shows two of these ways people share culture. Add your page to the book.

- food, clothing, and shelter
- language
- music and dance
- art
- celebrations

## Visit Your Library

**Madlenka** by Peter Sis. Neighbors share their culture with Madlenka.

**Something's Happening on Calabash Street** by Judith Enderle and Stephanie Jacob Gordon. People on Calabash Street share special meals.

**Emeka's Gift: An African Counting Story** by Ifeoma Onyefulu. Read about the Igala tribe in Nigeria, Africa.

# Looking Back

A "cityscape"
ceramic clock, 1925

# Looking Back

❝Study the past if you would discover the future.❞

—Chinese proverb

## Preview the Content

As you read, think about important things that have happened in the United States. At the end of this unit, finish the chart. Show what happened in the correct order.

America's History

First ➡ Next ➡ Last

**change** To become different. (page 175)

**season** One of four parts of the year that have different kinds of weather. (page 175)

**history** The story of what has happened in the past. (page 178)

Our country old and new.

**hero** A person who has done something brave or important. (page 206)

**technology** New inventions used in everyday life. (page 210)

# Four Generations

by Mary Ann Hoberman

illustrated by Russ Wilson

Sometimes when we go out for walks,
I listen while my father talks.

The thing he talks of most of all
Is how it was when he was small

And he went walking with <u>his</u> dad
And conversations that they had

About <u>his</u> father and the talks
They had when <u>they</u> went out for walks.

## Think About It

1 Who are the people in this poem?

2 What are some things you talk about with your family?

### Start the Unit Project

**A Community History Quilt**
Your class will make a quilt that shows the history of your community. As you read this unit, think about the stories people tell about changes in people and places. Look for new ways people learn to do things.

### Use Technology

**GO ONLINE** Visit The Learning Site at **www.harcourtschool.com/ socialstudies** for additional activities, primary sources, and other resources to use in this unit.

# Time and Change

**Main Idea**
Things change all the time.

**Vocabulary**

yesterday

today

tomorrow

change

season

You can talk about time in different ways. **Yesterday** I got a new shirt. **Today** in school I am learning about time. **Tomorrow** I will go bowling.

today

yesterday

tomorrow

Things change over time. To **change** is to become different. We see things change in spring, summer, fall, and winter. Each of these times is called a **season**.

spring

summer

fall

winter

LESSON 1
Review

1 **Vocabulary** What are the four **seasons**?

2 What are some things that have changed since the beginning of the school year?

3 List some things you did yesterday and today. Then list things you would like to do tomorrow.

# Use a Time Line

## ▶ Why It Matters

We need ways to show how things change over time.

## ▶ What You Need to Know

A **time line** shows when things happened and in what order. A time line can show days, weeks, years, or more. You read a time line from left to right. The things on the left happened first.

0   1   2   3

Samuel is born

Birthday party

176

# Practice the Skill

**1** Look at Samuel's time line. When did Samuel hit his first ball?

**2** What happened last on the time line?

**3** What happened when Samuel was two?

# Apply What You Learned

Make a time line of your school day.

First baseball hit

4　　　5　　　6

First day of school

Family vacation

# Trace a Family History

**Main Idea**
Families share their history through stories.

**Vocabulary**
history

Each family has its own history. **History** is made up of the stories people tell about what has happened.

Grandpa Ryan's photographs show our family history. He tells me about them.

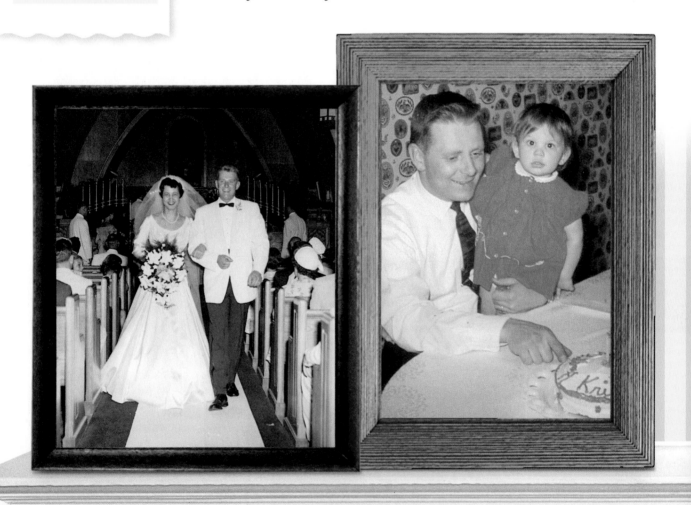

"When I married your grandma, most photographs were black and white.

We celebrated your mother's first birthday with a party.

We were proud when your mother finished high school.

Your mother and father met in college. They married after they finished college.

This is the very first photograph of you."

Grandma Bridgette came to the United States from Germany when she was young. She likes to show me the things she brought with her. She tells me a story about each one.

"This clock has been in my family for many years. It was made by my great-great-grandfather. One day it will belong to you."

## Clocks

People have kept track of time in many ways. Early people told time by where the sun, moon, or stars were in the sky. Some people used an hourglass. This tool is filled with sand. It takes exactly one hour for the sand to fall from the top to the bottom.

**LESSON 2**
**Review**

❶ **Vocabulary**   What is a family's **history**?

❷ Why do you think people retell family stories?

❸ Interview a classmate to learn his or her favorite family story.

181

# Use a Diagram

Vocabulary

diagram

## ▶ Why It Matters

One way to show a family history is with a diagram. A **diagram** is a drawing that shows parts of something.

## ▶ What You Need to Know

This diagram is called a family tree. It shows the parts of a family. You read the diagram starting from the bottom. As you go up the tree, you go farther back in a family's history.

## ▶ Practice the Skill

**1** Look at the diagram of the family tree. Where can you find the youngest people?

**2** Who are the people on the top row of the tree?

**3** Who are Dad's parents?

Grandma Bridgette  Grandpa Ryan  Grandma Anna  Grandpa John

Mom  Dad

Me

## ▶ Apply What You Learned

Make a family tree of your family or another family you know.

# A Community History

**Main Idea**
Like people, places also grow and change over time.

**Vocabulary**

past

present

future

Every community and state has changed. Each place has its own history.

This is Wilmington, North Carolina, in the **past**, or the time before now.

This is Wilmington in the **present**, or now.
There are more homes and new stores.

Wilmington will keep changing in the
**future**, or the time to come.

Leaders start communities
and help change them.

**Pennsylvania**

William Penn started what
is now Pennsylvania.
He wanted people to have
a place where they could
follow their own religion.

**Philadelphia, Pennsylvania, 1683**

James Oglethorpe wanted a place where people could start over. He and others from England started Savannah, Georgia.

**Georgia**

Stephen F. Austin brought Americans to live in Texas. Many Americans living in the East were looking for new lands farther west.

**Texas**

**LESSON 3**
**Review**

1. **Vocabulary** How can you learn about the **past**?

2. How has Wilmington changed from past to present?

3. Write a paragraph about something that has changed in your community.

# Identify Cause and Effect

| Vocabulary |
| --- |
| cause |
| effect |

cause

## ▶ Why It Matters

Sometimes we need to explain why something happened. This helps us understand the past. It also helps us predict what will happen in the future.

## ▶ What You Need to Know

A **cause** is what makes something happen. An **effect** is what happens because of a cause.

## ▶ Practice the Skill

❶ Look at the two pictures. What happens first?

❷ Does the effect happen before or after the cause?

❸ What is the effect?

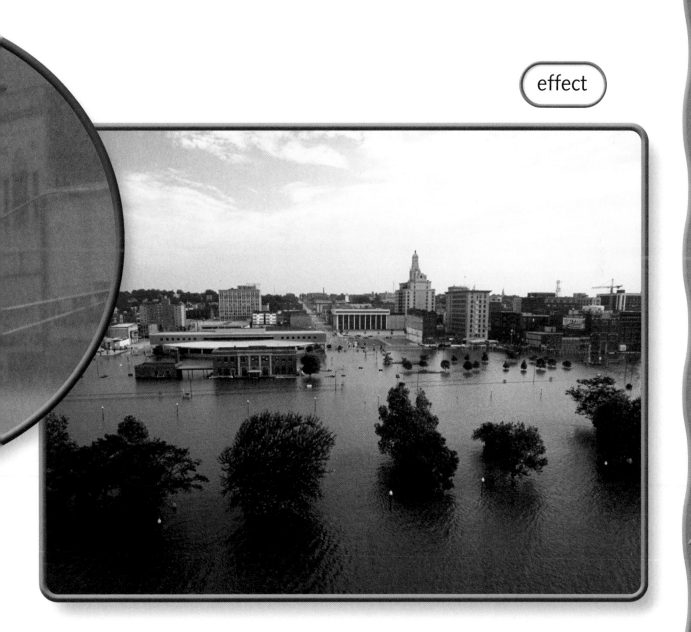

## ▶ Apply What You Learned

People build new homes, schools, and stores in communities. What might be the causes for this? What might be the effects on people living there?

# America's First People

**Main Idea**
Many groups lived in North and South America before Columbus arrived.

**Vocabulary**

explorer

**Nez Perce**

**Mandan**

**Pomo**

**Hopi**

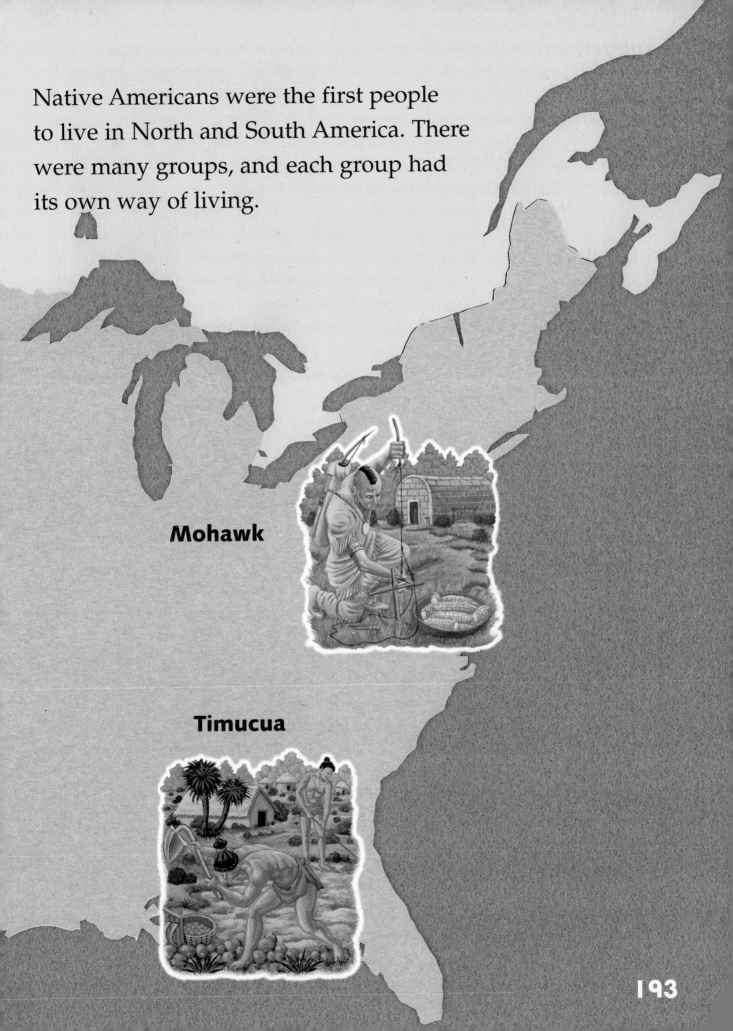

Native Americans were the first people to live in North and South America. There were many groups, and each group had its own way of living.

**Mohawk**

**Timucua**

Explorers came from other countries to North and South America. An **explorer** is a person who finds out about new land. Christopher Columbus was an explorer who sailed from Spain in 1492. Columbus was looking for a new way to get to Asia.

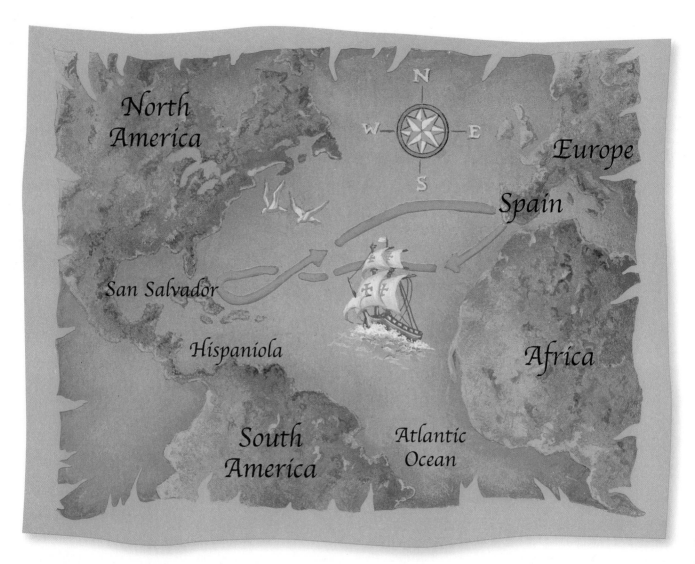

Columbus and his crew sailed for many days. Finally they landed on the beach of an island in North America. They met the Taino people who lived there.

When Columbus returned to Spain, he told people about the islands he had found. Soon many more people crossed the ocean to explore North and South America.

**LESSON 4
Review**

1 **Vocabulary** Which **explorer** came to North America in 1492?

2 Why do you think explorers want to find out about new lands?

3 Read about an early Native American group. Write a short report telling how they lived.

# 5 Our Country's History

## Main Idea
Our country's history is made up of many people and the things they did.

### Vocabulary
settler

freedom

Long ago, people from far away began moving to North America. One group was the Pilgrims. They were **settlers**, or people who wanted to make a home in a new place. The Pilgrims sailed from England on a ship called the <u>Mayflower</u>.

**FAST FACT** One child was born on the <u>Mayflower</u> during the Pilgrims' journey. His parents named him Oceanus.

Many native people lived in North America. The Wampanoags were the native people who lived where the Pilgrims landed. A Wampanoag man named Squanto lived with the Pilgrims. He showed them how to grow corn.

The Pilgrims were thankful for a good harvest. They celebrated with a great feast. Some Wampanoags came to this celebration. Today we remember this feast with a holiday called Thanksgiving.

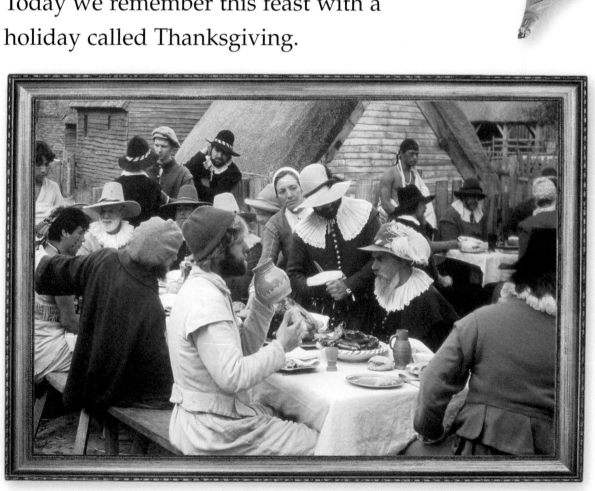

More settlers came to North America. The land here belonged to England, and the people had to follow England's laws. They thought some of the laws were unfair.

On July 4, 1776, American leaders signed the Declaration of Independence. It told the King of England that Americans wanted to be free.

Americans fought a war for **freedom**, or the right to make choices. Today we celebrate our freedom with parades, picnics, and fireworks. This holiday is called Independence Day. It is our country's birthday.

Let freedom ring!

**LESSON 5**
**Review**

1. **Vocabulary** Who are **settlers**?

2. Describe the reasons we celebrate Thanksgiving and Independence Day.

3. Draw pictures to show how people celebrate these holidays.

# Celebrating History

**Main Idea**
We celebrate on holidays to remember our history.

**Vocabulary**

veteran

peace

Thanksgiving and Independence Day are important American holidays. We celebrate our history on other holidays, too.

On Dr. Martin Luther King, Jr., Day, we honor a man who worked to make things fair for all Americans. He made speeches asking for equal rights for everyone.

Presidents' Day started as Washington's Birthday. It was a holiday to remember our first President. Now it is a day to remember the work of all our Presidents.

. BIOGRAPHY .

### Abraham Lincoln 1809–1865
**Character Trait: Self-discipline**

Abraham Lincoln's family was poor. He could not go to school, so he studied at home. He became a lawyer and later President of the United States.

**GO ONLINE**

MULTIMEDIA BIOGRAPHIES
Visit The Learning Site at **www.harcourtschool.com/biographies** to learn about other famous people.

On Memorial Day we remember the people who died in wars for our country.

We are proud of the flag of our country. On Flag Day, people fly the flag from their homes.

On Veterans Day we think about the men and women who have fought in past wars. A **veteran** is someone who has served in the military. We give thanks for **peace**, a time of quietness and calm.

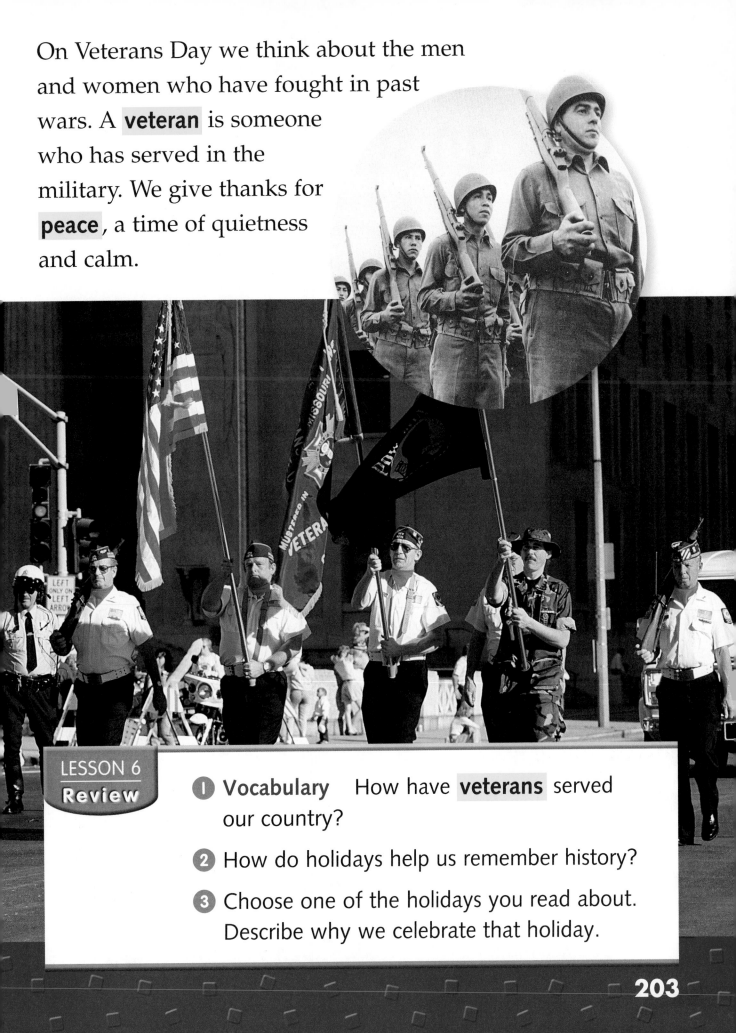

**LESSON 6**
**Review**

1 **Vocabulary** How have **veterans** served our country?

2 How do holidays help us remember history?

3 Choose one of the holidays you read about. Describe why we celebrate that holiday.

# Follow a Route on a Map

Vocabulary

route

## ▶ Why It Matters

Routes on a map show us how to get from one place to another.

## ▶ What You Need to Know

Think about the school bus drivers who pick up children for school. They follow a route. A **route** is a path that leads from one place to another.

## ▶ Practice the Skill

❶ Look at the map of the parade route. How is the parade route shown?

❷ Where will the parade start?

❸ In which direction will the parade go on Third Avenue?

❹ What will it pass on Pine Street?

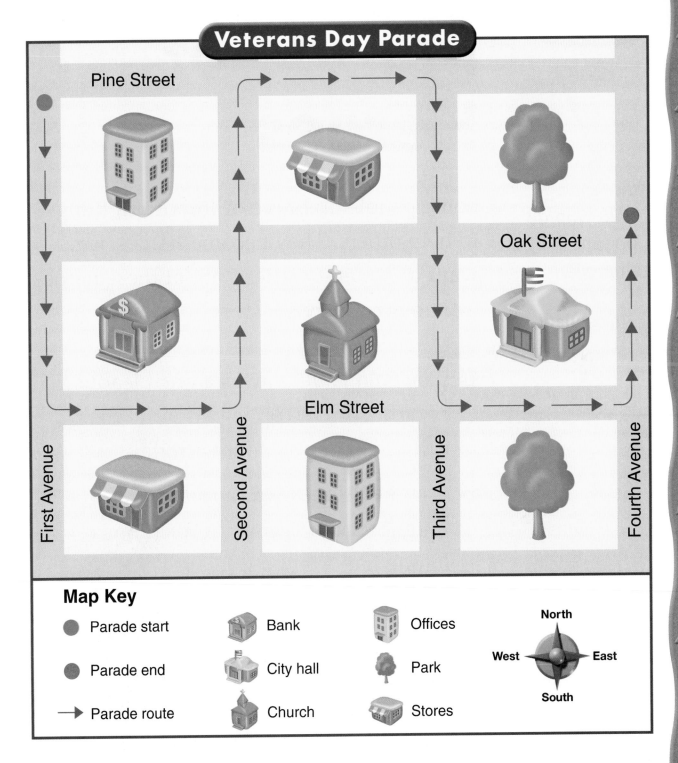

**Veterans Day Parade**

Pine Street

Oak Street

First Avenue

Second Avenue

Elm Street

Third Avenue

Fourth Avenue

**Map Key**

- ● Parade start
- ● Parade end
- → Parade route
- Bank
- City hall
- Church
- Offices
- Park
- Stores

North
West — East
South

# ▶ Apply What You Learned

Make a map of your community. Show the
route you follow from home to school.

Practice your map and globe skills
with the **GeoSkills CD-ROM.**

# Parade of Heroes

**Main Idea**
People who do important things are heroes.

**Vocabulary**

**hero**

Some people do brave or important things to help others. They become **heroes** we want to remember. Read about these heroes from our country's history.

1. **Benjamin Franklin** was a great leader of our country. He helped write the rules our country follows today.

2. **John Paul Jones** was a sailor who fought for our country's freedom. In one important battle, his ships fought against larger ships and won.

**3** **Molly Pitcher** also fought for freedom. She gave thirsty soldiers water. She also helped the soldiers fire the cannon.

**4** **Phillis Wheatley** wrote poetry. One of her poems is about George Washington. She believed he was a great leader.

**5** **Sequoyah** was a Cherokee Indian. He wanted his people to be able to read and write their language. He made up an alphabet for them to use.

**6** **Jane Addams** started a community center called Hull-House in Chicago. People who came from other countries could learn English and job skills there.

**7** **Ida B. Wells** wrote about the ways African Americans were being treated unfairly. She wanted people to know the truth so things would change.

**8** **George Washington Carver** showed farmers that planting peanuts made their soil better. He also found many uses for peanuts.

**9** **Orville and Wilbur Wright** were brothers who were interested in flying. They worked together to make and fly one of the first airplanes.

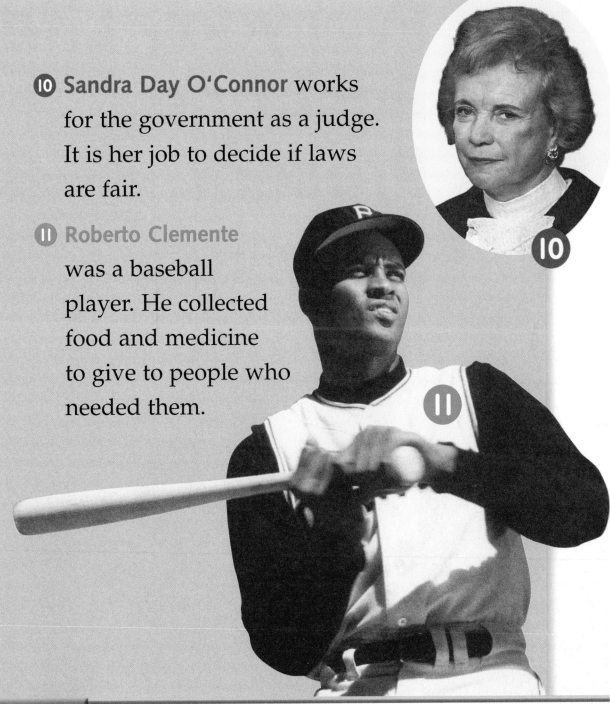

**10** Sandra Day O'Connor works for the government as a judge. It is her job to decide if laws are fair.

**11** Roberto Clemente was a baseball player. He collected food and medicine to give to people who needed them.

LESSON 7
Review

**1** **Vocabulary** Why are some people **heroes**?

**2** What other heroes do you know about?

**3** Compare two people from this lesson. Tell how the things these heroes did are the same and different.

**209**

# Everyday Life, Past and Present

**Main Idea**
Technology has changed many ways of doing things.

**Vocabulary**
technology
transportation
communication
recreation

When you wear clean clothes, ride to school, play a video game, or talk on the phone, you are using technology. **Technology** is all of the helpful inventions we use. Technology is always changing.

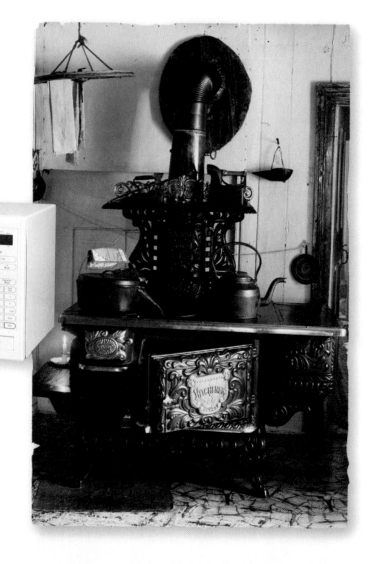

# Household Tools

People are always making new tools to make daily chores easier.

## Thomas Alva Edison  1847–1931
### Character Trait: Inventiveness

Thomas Edison wanted a better kind of light than candles and gas lamps. He made an electric lightbulb. At first only a few homes had this new technology. Now people around the world use electric light.

MULTIMEDIA BIOGRAPHIES
Visit The Learning Site at **www.harcourtschool.com/biographies** to learn about other famous people.

# Transportation

**Transportation** is ways of carrying people and things from place to place. People use transportation on land, on water, and in the air.

Airplanes today carry many passengers.

Bicycles have changed greatly over time.

Trains are the fastest way for people to travel on land.

Long ago, families traveled in covered wagons.

Early explorers traveled by ship to find new places.

213

# Communication

Every day, people talk or write to share their ideas and feelings. This sharing is called **communication**.

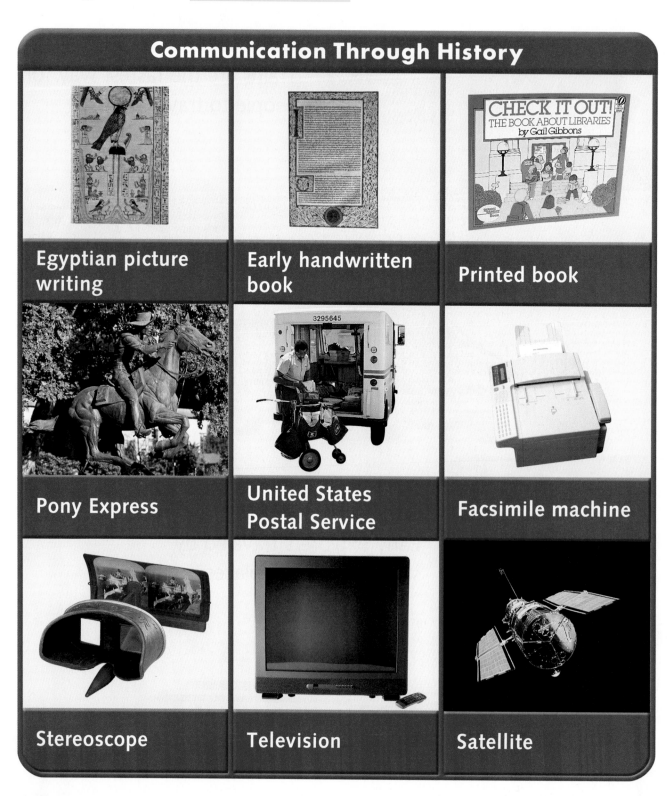

## Communication Through History

**Egyptian picture writing**

**Early handwritten book**

**Printed book**

**Pony Express**

**United States Postal Service**

**Facsimile machine**

**Stereoscope**

**Television**

**Satellite**

# Recreation

People like to relax in their spare time. **Recreation** is anything people do to have fun.

Long ago, people watched plays in large outdoor theaters. These theaters were made so people in the top rows could hear the actors.

---

**LESSON 8**
**Review**

❶ **Vocabulary**   How do you use **technology** at school?

❷ Describe how technology has changed transportation, communication, and recreation.

❸ Make a poster. Show more household tools that have changed the ways families do chores.

# The Telephone

The telephone makes it easy for people to communicate. It was invented by Alexander Graham Bell. The first telephone call was from Bell to his helper in another room. Now we can use the telephone to talk with people around the world.

**1** How do you think these early telephones were used?

**2** How has the telephone changed?

## Activity

Choose another communication tool, such as the radio. Find out how it has changed over time.

## Research

Visit The Learning Site at
**www.harcourtschool.com/primarysources**
to research other primary sources.

# VISIT Old Sturbridge Village

## Get Ready

Old Sturbridge Village is a good place to learn about the past. Actors dress up like the people who lived there more than a hundred years ago. They do the jobs those people did so visitors can see what life was like then.

## What to See

**1** Blacksmiths shape hot metal with hammers to make and repair tools.

**2** Children play rounders in a field. Rounders is a game like baseball.

**3** Children help their mother with home chores such as sewing.

**4** Shoemakers use wooden pegs or thread to put the soles onto shoes.

## Take a Field Trip

**A VIRTUAL TOUR**
Visit The Learning Site at
**www.harcourtschool.com/tours**
to take virtual tours of other
historic sites.

**A VIDEO TOUR**

Check your media
center or classroom library
for a video featuring a segment
from Reading Rainbow.

# Review and Test Preparation

## Visual Summary

Put these events in the correct order in the chart.

- Explorers came to North America.
- Pilgrims moved to North America.
- Native Americans lived in North and South America.

**America's History**

| First | → | Next | → | Last |
|-------|---|------|---|------|

**THINK & WRITE**

**Draw a Picture**  Think about a change that has happened in your family. Draw a picture of it.

**Write a Letter**  Write to a friend or family member. Tell about the change shown in your picture.

## Use Vocabulary

Give another example to explain each word.

| | Word | Examples | |
|---|---|---|---|
| **1** | change (p. 175) | A new teacher at school | |
| **2** | season (p. 175) | Summer | |
| **3** | history (p. 178) | The Pilgrims give thanks | |
| **4** | hero (p. 206) | Abraham Lincoln | |
| **5** | technology (p. 210) | Electric light | |

## Recall Facts

**6** What kinds of changes happen with the seasons?

**7** In what year did Christopher Columbus sail to North America?

**8** Why did Americans fight to be free from England?

**9** Which holiday celebrates our country's birthday?

   **A** Presidents' Day      **C** Flag Day

   **B** Memorial Day     **D** Independence Day

**10** For which of these is a bicycle used?

   **F** information      **H** communication

   **G** transportation    **J** history

**11** How is our Thanksgiving holiday the same as the Pilgrims' Thanksgiving? How is it different?

**12** How would your life be different if there were no telephones?

## Apply Chart and Graph Skills

**13** How much time is shown on the time line?

**14** In what month was Theodore Roosevelt born?

**15** Which two Presidents were born in the same month?

**16** George W. Bush was born in July. Would you put his birthday before or after Thomas Jefferson's?

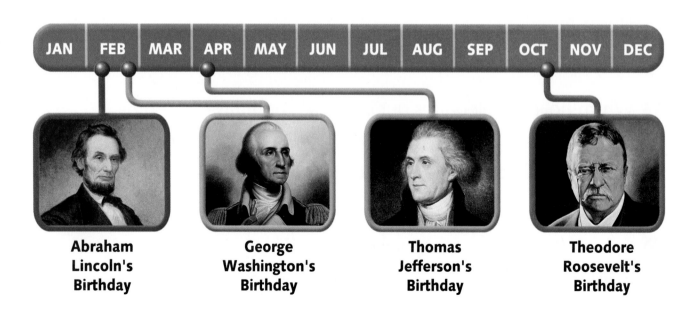

| JAN | FEB | MAR | APR | MAY | JUN | JUL | AUG | SEP | OCT | NOV | DEC |

Abraham Lincoln's Birthday

George Washington's Birthday

Thomas Jefferson's Birthday

Theodore Roosevelt's Birthday

**17** On which bus route is the city hall?

**18** Which bus route goes along Fifth Avenue?

**19** Does bus route 2 pass through the west or the east part of town?

**20** Which bus route could you take to go to the museum from Third Avenue?

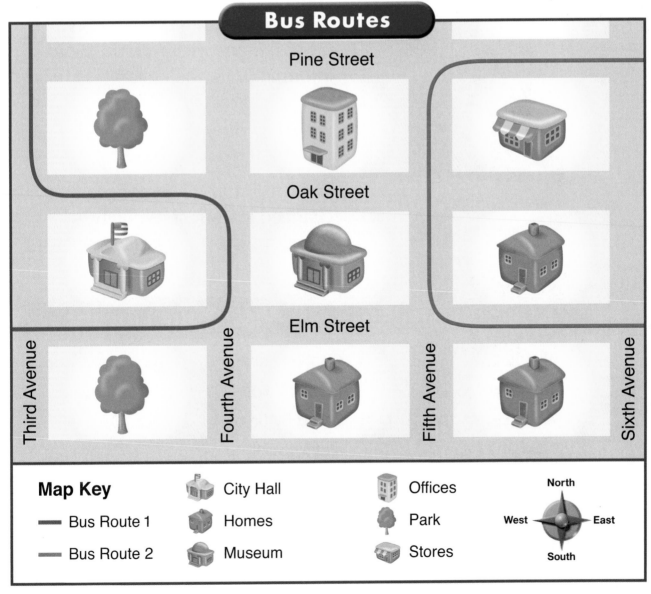

**Bus Routes**

Pine Street

Oak Street

Elm Street

Third Avenue

Fourth Avenue

Fifth Avenue

Sixth Avenue

**Map Key**

— Bus Route 1
— Bus Route 2

City Hall
Homes
Museum

Offices
Park
Stores

North
West — East
South

# Unit Activities

**GO ONLINE**

Visit The Learning Site at **www.harcourtschool.com/ socialstudies/activities** for additional activities.

**Complete the Unit Project** Work with your group to finish the unit project. Decide how you will show the history of your community in your quilt.

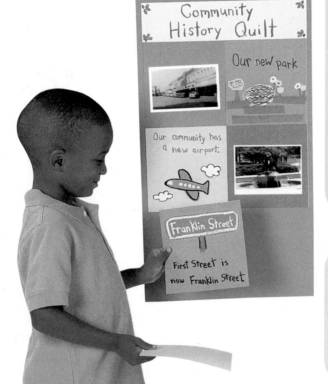

## Interview a Family Member

Write some questions you want to ask a family member about your community's history. Then interview the family member. Write down his or her answers. Add the new information to the quilt.

## Showing Change

Draw a picture of something that has changed in your community.

- buildings   - roads   - places

## Visit Your Library

**This Is the Turkey** by Abby Levine. Max and his family prepare a Thanksgiving meal for family and friends.

**On the Day the Tall Ships Sailed** by Betty and Michael Paraskevas. A bald eagle flies above New York City during an Independence Day celebration.

**The Piano Man** by Debbie Chocolate. A granddaughter retells her grandfather's stories about playing the piano for the silent movies.

# Jobs People Do

A toy tool chest, 1910

# Jobs
# People Do

A toy tool chest,
1910

6

# Jobs People Do

66 There is no substitute for hard work. 99

—Thomas Edison, *Life*, 1932

## Preview the Content

As you read, look for main ideas about jobs people do. At the end of this unit, write a sentence to summarize, or tell in a few words, what the unit is about.

Main Idea      Main Idea

Summary Sentence

**goods** Things that can be bought and sold. (page 240)

**services** Work done for others for money. (page 242)

Earn and spend.

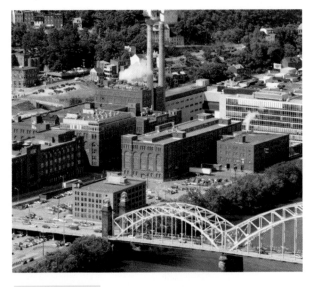

**factory** A building in which people use machines to make goods. (page 244)

**market** A place where people buy and sell goods. (page 258)

**trade** To exchange one thing for another. (page 268)

# Rush Hour

by Christine Loomis
illustrated by Mari Takabayashi

Find out what jobs people
do in this busy city.

Alarms are buzzing,
Day is dawning,
Sleepy people
Wake up yawning.

Showers splash,
Teeth are brushed,
Hair is combed,
Breakfast rushed.

Out their doors
Go moms and dads,
Lugging tools
Or books and pads.

Some alone,
Some with strollers,
Walkers, runners,
Readers, rollers,

Running, jumping
Onto trains,
Subways, buses,
Boats, and planes,

Taxis, bikes,
A car-pool van,
Cars of blue and red and tan.
Engines start up with a jerk.
People hurry off to work.

Horns go beep-beep, whistles blow,
Planes go fast, trucks go slow.
Trolleys sway, ferries rock,
Time keeps ticking on the clock.

Cars on side streets,
Trains on tracks,
Whizzing,
Zipping,
Clicky
Clack,

Rumbling,
Roaring,
Jiggling,
Jumping,

Left turn,
Right turn,
Backing,
Bumping.

Through the tunnels,
On the highways,
Over bridges,
Roads, and byways,
Down the river,
In the air,
People rushing everywhere!

In a blink
They disappear.
Trains are empty,
Tunnels clear.
Streets are quiet,
No more mobs.

# People have begun their jobs.

When day is over,
Each job ends.
Workers wave
Good-bye to friends.

Then they race
To catch the trains,
Subways, buses,
Boats, and planes,
Taxis, bikes,
A car-pool van,
Cars of blue and red
and tan.

Down the river,
Underground,
Traffic creeping
Homeward bound.
Over bridges,
Roads, and byways,
Through the tunnels,
On the highways,

Right turn,
Left turn,
Backing,
Bumping,
Roaring,
Rumbling,
Jiggling,
Jumping,

Whizzing,
Zipping,
Clicky
Clack,
Cars on side streets,
Trains on tracks.

Horns go beep-beep,
Whistles blow.

Nighttime lights
Begin to glow.

Doors swing open.
Kids run fast.

Moms and dads
Are home at last.

238

# Think About It

1. How are the workers in this book the same as workers in your community? How are they different?

2. Draw a picture of yourself doing a job you would like to do.

## Read a Book

Jobs of the Past

## Start the Unit Project

**Event Pamphlet** Your class will make a pamphlet about an event at your school. As you read this unit, think about how people work together to complete a job.

## Use Technology

Visit The Learning Site at **www.harcourtschool.com/ socialstudies** for additional activities, primary sources, and other resources to use in this unit.

# Goods and Services

**Main Idea**
People depend on one another for goods and services.

Just like the people in <u>Rush Hour</u>, the people in your community are busy working every day. Some make goods. **Goods** are things that people make and sell.

pizza maker

240

furniture maker

potter

bakers

dressmaker

241

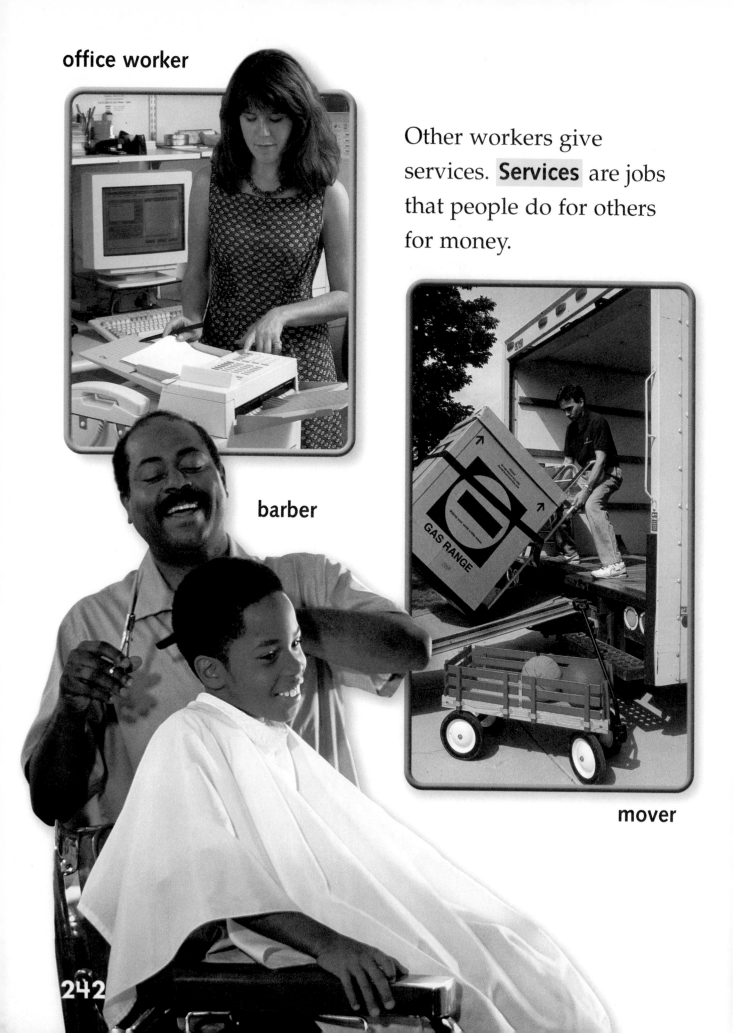

office worker

Other workers give services. **Services** are jobs that people do for others for money.

barber

mover

242

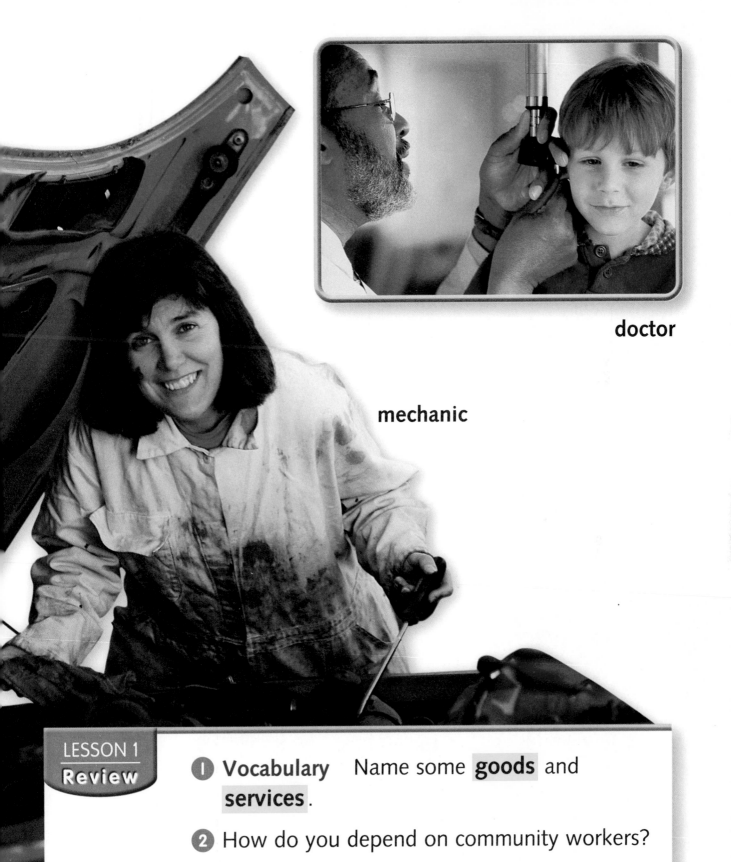

doctor

mechanic

**LESSON 1**
**Review**

① **Vocabulary**   Name some **goods** and **services**.

② How do you depend on community workers?

③ Make a table showing goods and services you use.

243

# 2

# A Pencil Factory

**Main Idea**
People work together to make goods in a factory.

**Vocabulary**

**factory**

Think about the pencil you use to write with. Resources are needed to make pencils. It also takes many people working together to make them. The pencils are made in a factory. A **factory** is a building in which people use machines to make goods.

Wood is needed for the pencils, so loggers cut down trees. Truck drivers take the logs to the factory. Later, foresters will plant new trees.

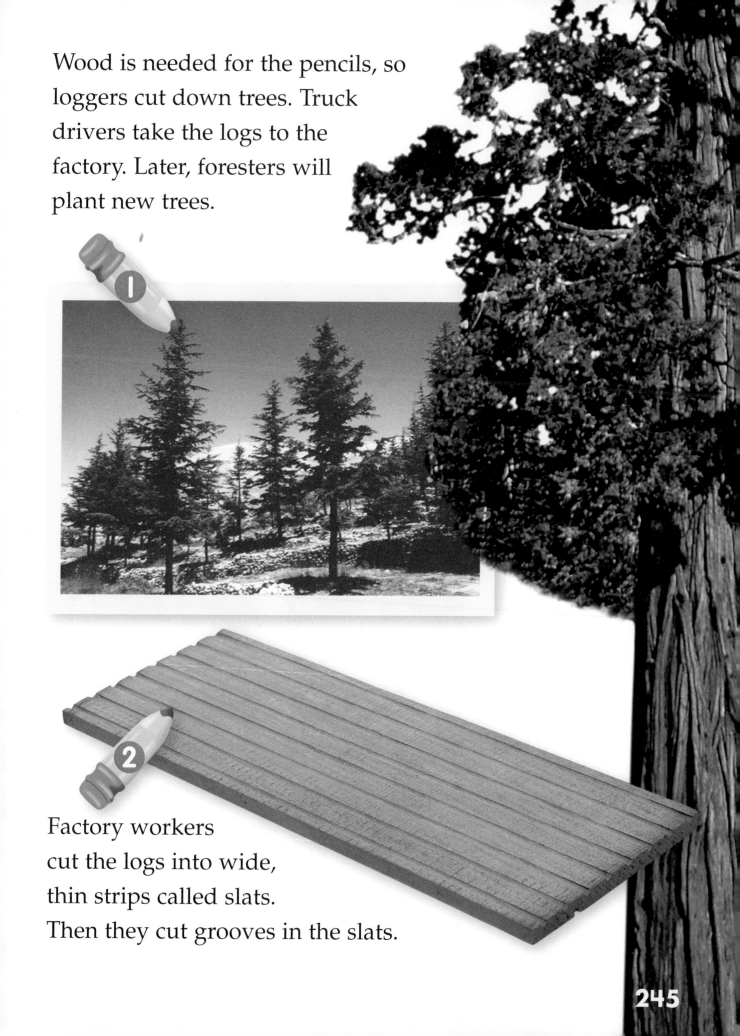

Factory workers cut the logs into wide, thin strips called slats. Then they cut grooves in the slats.

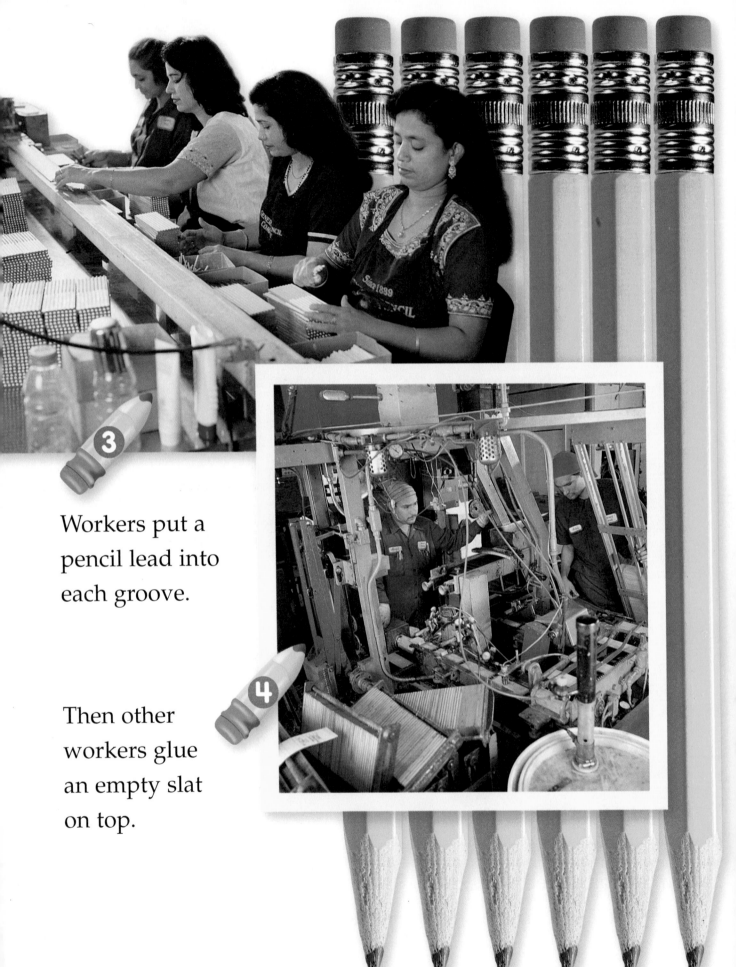

**3** Workers put a pencil lead into each groove.

**4** Then other workers glue an empty slat on top.

246

More workers cut the slat into separate pencils.

In another part of the factory, the pencils are painted.

More workers add
erasers to the pencils.
At last the pencils are
ready to be taken to
stores and sold.

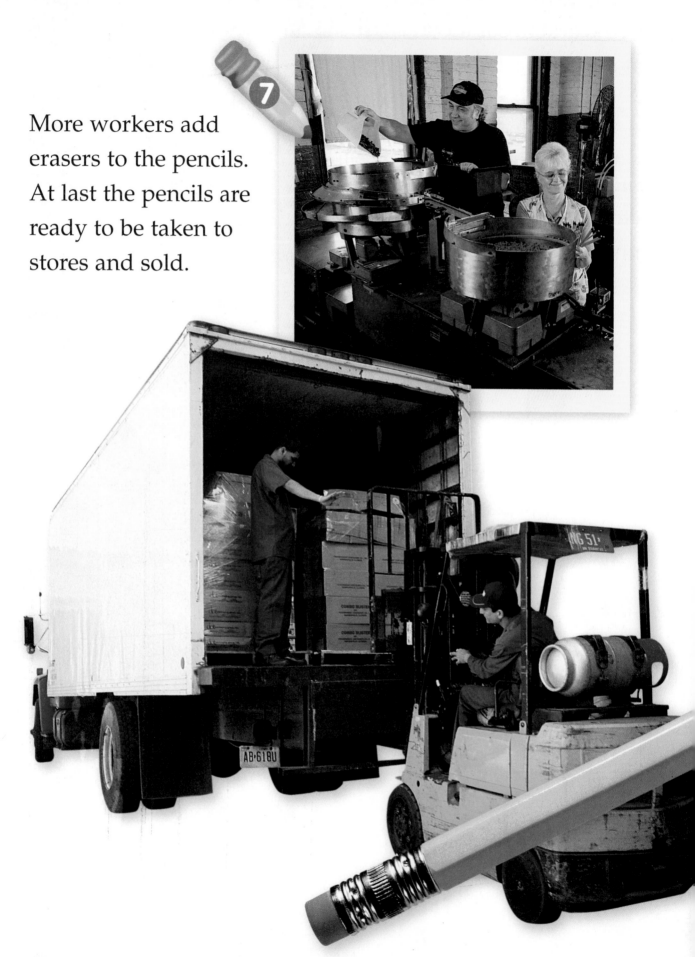

## Graphite from China

The best graphite for pencil lead first came from China. Pencils made with it were painted yellow, a color used by Chinese leaders. This showed that these pencils were made with the best graphite.

**LESSON 2 Review**

1 **Vocabulary** What is a **factory**?

2 How do people work together to make something?

3 Write a paragraph to describe what makes a good worker.

**Skills**

**CHART AND GRAPH**

# Use a Picture Graph

**Vocabulary**

picture graph

## ▶ Why It Matters

A **picture graph** is a chart that uses pictures
to show how many there are of something.
The key tells you what each picture stands for.

## ▶ What You Need to Know

The title tells you what the chart is about.
The pencil symbol in the key stands for one
box of pencils. Look at each row from left
to right to see how many boxes were sold
on each day.

# ▶ Practice the Skill

**❶** Look at the picture graph. For how many days were the pencils sold?

**❷** How many boxes were sold on Friday?

**❸** On which day were the most boxes sold?

**❹** Were more boxes sold on Wednesday or Thursday?

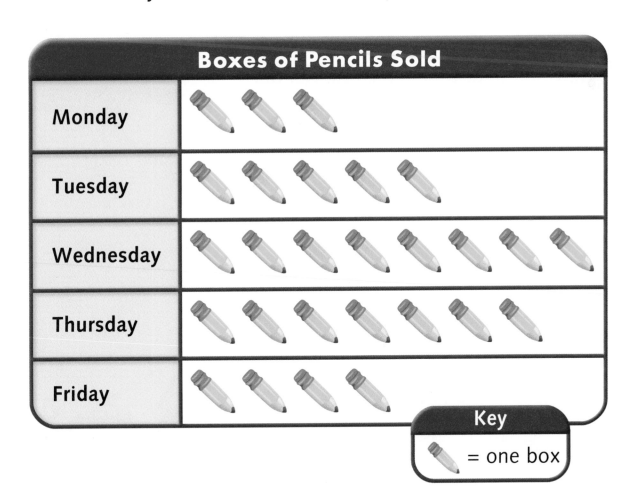

# ▶ Apply What You Learned

Make a picture graph to show how many books you read each day for one week.

# Why People Work

**Main Idea**
People work
to earn money
to buy what
they need.

**Vocabulary**

business

money

volunteer

Mr. Taylor has his own business. A **business** is an activity in which people make or sell goods or give services. They do this to earn money. Mr. Taylor uses the **money** he earns to buy the goods and services he needs.

One of Mr. Taylor's jobs is to help people plan their gardens. Sometimes he is a volunteer at schools, helping children plant gardens. When he is a **volunteer**, he does not get paid for his work.

**LESSON 3**
**Review**

❶ **Vocabulary** How do people use **money**?

❷ Why might someone be a volunteer?

❸ Find a picture of someone who is working. Write a sentence about the picture.

# Jobs Change

**Main Idea**
The kinds of work people do and the ways they do them change over time.

**Vocabulary**

**robot**

New technology can change the way people work. It can make their work easier and help them work faster. Sometimes they may need to learn a new way of doing their job.

New technology has ended some old jobs. Grocery stores now have freezers and refrigerators. Workers are no longer needed to deliver ice and milk to people's homes. Special workers are no longer needed to run elevators.

**RAILROAD BRAKEMEN**
Rate $1.94¾ per hour; A-1 reference only. Apply 8 a. m. to 11 a. m. Monday through Friday at employment office, Union Railroad Co., 664 Linden Ave., East Pittsburgh.

New technology has made some new jobs. People use robots in factories. A **robot** is a machine that can do a job. It is run by a computer. Many office workers use computers, too.

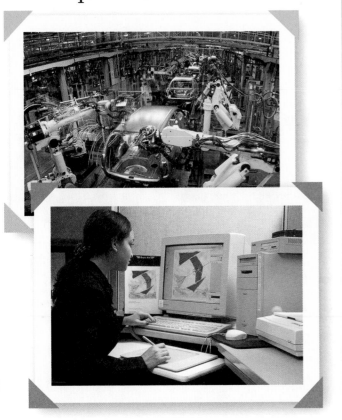

·BIOGRAPHY·

**Ellen Ochoa**
**born in 1955**
**Character Trait:**
**Cooperation**

Ellen Ochoa is an astronaut. She has gone into space several times. On one trip she and other astronauts took goods to the International Space Station.

MULTIMEDIA BIOGRAPHIES
Visit The Learning Site at
**www.harcourtschool.com/biographies**
to learn about other famous people.

**GO ONLINE**

**LESSON 4**
**Review**

1 **Vocabulary** How do people use **robots** at work?

2 Describe how technology has changed the way people work.

3 Design a machine that could help you do a job.

# Buyers and Sellers

**Main Idea**
People can be buyers or sellers or both.

**Vocabulary**

market

save

Our community has a large outdoor market. A **market** is a place where people buy and sell goods.

Today I have money to spend at the market. I am going to use it to buy a birthday present for my brother.

The sellers at the market use some of the money they earn to buy things they need. They **save**, or keep, some money to use later. They put this money in the bank. A bank is a business that keeps money safe for people.

Save for the future.

LESSON 5
Review

❶ **Vocabulary**   What do people do at a **market**?

❷ What can you do with money you do not spend?

❸ Draw a map of a market. Show six places shoppers might spend money.

# Use a Bar Graph

## ▶ Why It Matters

Some kinds of information are easier to find on a bar graph. A **bar graph** uses bars to show how much or how many.

## ▶ What You Need to Know

The title of a graph tells you what it shows. This graph shows how many baskets of berries were sold at a market. The graph has rows that you look at from left to right. The picture shows the kind of berry. Each colored block stands for one basket of berries. The blocks show how many baskets were sold.

# ▶ Practice the Skill

**1** Look at the bar graph. Which kind of berry sold the most?

**2** Were more baskets of blackberries or raspberries sold?

**3** Which kind of berry sold the least?

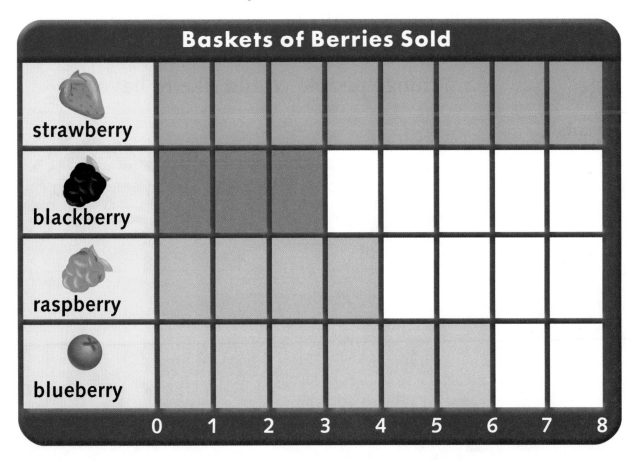

# ▶ Apply What You Learned

Make a bar graph to show the kinds of snack food the children in your class like to eat.

# Wanting More or Less

**Main Idea**
People must make choices about what they want.

**Vocabulary**

wants

The Jacobs family is buying a new house. They need some things for their home. They also want some things, such as a garage, a backyard, and a fireplace. **Wants** are things people would like to have.

They know they should not spend all of their money. They will need some for food, clothes, medical care, and other needs. They budget, or plan, for what they need. They use some of what is left for things they want.

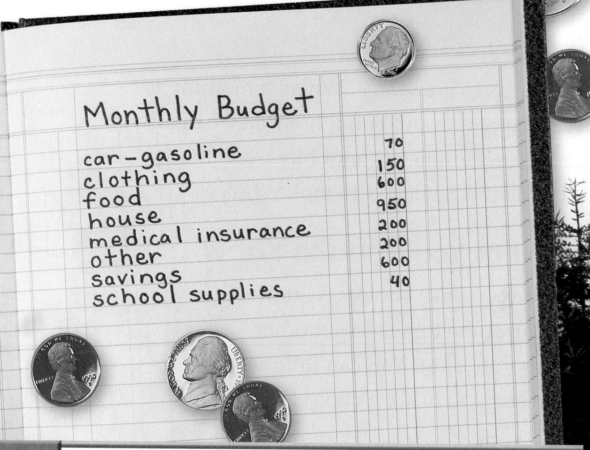

Monthly Budget

| | |
|---|---|
| car - gasoline | 70 |
| clothing | 150 |
| food | 600 |
| house | 950 |
| medical insurance | 200 |
| other | 200 |
| savings | 600 |
| school supplies | 40 |

**LESSON 6**
**Review**

1. **Vocabulary** What are some **wants** people have?

2. What must families think about before they spend their money?

3. Cut out pictures from magazines or catalogs. Make a collage of things people want.

## Skills

### CITIZENSHIP

# Make Choices When Buying

Vocabulary

scarce

## ▶ Why It Matters

Some things are scarce. When something is scarce, there is not enough. Money can also be scarce. Families cannot buy everything they want. They need to make choices.

## ▶ What You Need to Know

When you make choices, you must give up some things to get other things you want. You can follow these steps to make a choice.

**Step 1** Decide if the choices are needs or wants.

**Step 2** Think about what you would give up to get each choice.

**Step 3** Make a choice.

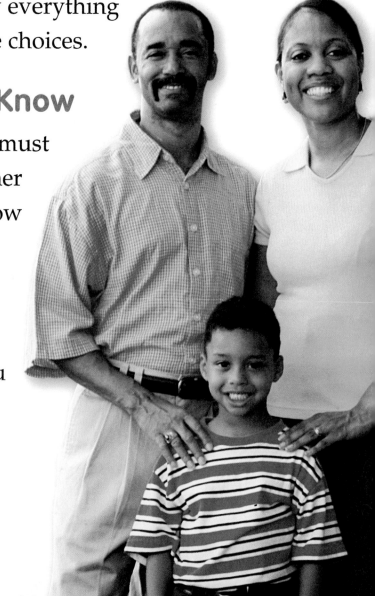

## ▶ Practice the Skill

**1** Study the pictures to see how the Jacobs family is thinking of spending their money.

**2** Follow the steps. Decide what choice you think the family should make.

**3** Tell why you think the family should make that choice.

## ▶ Apply What You Learned

Shop with your family, and talk about the choices your family makes.

# Trading with Others

**Main Idea**
People around the world depend on one another.

**Vocabulary**

trade

We trade for things that we want or need. When we **trade**, we give one thing to get another thing.

**People trade with money.**

JACK'S LEMONADE

**People trade services.**

**People trade goods.**

**FAST FACT** The 1909 Honus Wagner baseball trading card is so scarce, it sold for more than a million dollars!

Think about the goods you use every day. Many of these goods were made in other countries. People all over the world trade with one another.

MADE IN ITALY
HAND PAINTED

MADE IN CHINA

100% Cotton/Algodón
Machine wash cool with like colors
Use only non-chlorine bleach when needed
Tumble dry low
Lavar en lavadora con agua fría
con colores similares
Usar solamenté blanqueador sin cloro
Cuando se necesite
Made in India/Hecho en India
RN # 63232

Some goods are made in the United States with parts from other countries.

# A CLOSER LOOK
## Clothes from Around the World

You can find out what countries the United States trades with. Just look at the labels in your clothes! You'll see that your clothes come from countries around the world.

Why are some clothing labels written in several languages?

100% COTTON/COTON/ALGODON
MADE IN U.S.A./FABRIQUE AUX E-U
HECHO EN LOS E.U.A.

X LARGE/T GRAND/
X GRANDE

MACHINE WASH WARM IN LIKE COLORS.
LAVER A LA MACHINE A L'EAU TIEDE
AVEC COULEURS SEMBLABLES.
LAVAR A MANO O EN LAVADORA CON
AGUA TIBIA CON COLORES SIMILARES.

ONLY NON-CHLORINE BLEACH.
AGENT DE BLANCHIMENT SANS
CHLORURE SEULEMENT.
SOLO BLANQUEADOR SIN CLORO.

TUMBLE DRY MEDIUM.
SECHER A TEMPERATURE MOYENNE.
SECAR A TEMPERATURA BAJA.

DO NOT IRON IF DECORATED.
NE PAS REPASSER SI DECORE.
NO PLANCHAR SI TIENE ESTAMPADO.

RN 15763     CA 21356

Philippines

Canada

U.S.A.

China

Japan

Mexico

People take their goods to market in many ways. Some goods do not need to travel far. In Thailand, small boats carry foods and other goods to markets nearby.

Some goods are sent to markets in other countries. Ships and airplanes carry goods from the United States to markets around the world.

People everywhere trade their goods to get the things they need and want.

LESSON 7
Review

1 **Vocabulary** In what ways can people **trade** with one another?

2 How does trading help people around the world meet their needs?

3 Make a list of services or goods you can trade for services or goods you want.

# VISIT

# People at Work

## Get Ready

In a community, people have different jobs. Many people work in offices. Others have jobs outside. Some people wear uniforms to work. People are working everywhere.

Dentist

## What to See

Store clerk

Construction worker

Ballet teacher

Police officer

Architect

Taxi

Taxicab driver

## Take a Field Trip

**GO ONLINE**

**A VIRTUAL TOUR**
Visit The Learning Site at
**www.harcourtschool.com/tours**
to take virtual tours of
other occupations.

**READING RAINBOW.**

**A VIDEO TOUR**
Check your media
center or classroom library
for a video featuring a segment
from Reading Rainbow.

# 6 Review and Test Preparation

## Visual Summary

Write what you learned about the main ideas in this unit.

People make and sell goods.

People offer services.

**Summary Sentence**

**THINK & WRITE**

**Make a List**   List five workers you know about in your community.

**Write a Question**
Choose a worker. Write something you want to know about the job he or she does.

## Use Vocabulary

Fill in the blanks with the correct words.

People work together in a ❶_____ to make ketchup, mustard, and soup. When the ❷_____ are finished, they are put on trucks. The trucks take the goods to ❸_____, where they are sold. People ❹_____ money for goods at markets.

| |
|---|
| **goods** (p. 240) |
| **factory** (p. 244) |
| **markets** (p. 258) |
| **trade** (p. 268) |

## Recall Facts

❺ Name two services in your community that your family uses.

❻ What do people use to trade for goods and services?

❼ How does new technology change the ways people work?

❽ Why do people in one country trade goods with people in another country?

❾ Which of these workers makes goods?
**A** baker        **C** barber
**B** doctor       **D** bus driver

❿ Which of these is a want?
**F** sandwich     **H** television
**G** jacket       **J** house

⑪ What new jobs might there be in the future?

⑫ Why do you think people save money?

**Apply Chart and Graph Skills**

| Patients | |
|---|---|
| Monday | 🩺 🩺 🩺 |
| Tuesday | 🩺 🩺 🩺 🩺 🩺 🩺 |
| Wednesday | 🩺 🩺 |
| Thursday | 🩺 🩺 🩺 🩺 |
| Friday | 🩺 🩺 🩺 🩺 🩺 |

**Key**

🩺 = one patient

⑬ What does this picture graph show?

⑭ On which day did the doctor see the fewest patients?

⑮ On which day did the doctor see the most patients?

⑯ Did the doctor see more patients on Monday or on Thursday?

## Where Ryan's Shirts Come From

| | 0 | 1 | 2 | 3 | 4 | 5 | 6 | 7 |
|---|---|---|---|---|---|---|---|---|
| United States | | | | | | | | |
| Mexico | | | | | | | | |
| Taiwan | | | | | | | | |
| Italy | | | | | | | | |

**17** From which countries does Ryan have shirts?

**18** From which country does Ryan have the most shirts?

**19** Does Ryan have more shirts from the United States or from Taiwan?

**20** How many of Ryan's shirts are from Mexico?

# Unit Activities

**Complete the Unit Project** Work with your group to finish the unit project. Decide what information to put in your pamphlet.

**GO ONLINE**

Visit The Learning Site at www.harcourtschool.com/ socialstudies/activities for additional activities.

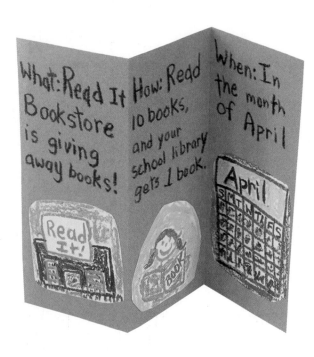

What: Read It Bookstore is giving away books!

How: Read 10 books, and your school library gets 1 book.

When: In the month of April

## Choose a Job

Choose one of the jobs needed to make the pamphlets.
- draw pictures
- write information
- fold pamphlets
- hand out pamphlets

## Write an Announcement

Think about how to invite people to the event. Make your pamphlet colorful. Remember to tell what, when, and where.

## Visit Your Library

**Market Day** by Lois Ehlert. See handmade items from around the world sold at a market.

**Messenger, Messenger** by Robert Burleigh. A bicycle messenger makes deliveries all over the city.

**When I'm Big** by Tim Drury. On a rainy day, a brother and sister imagine jobs they might have when they grow up.

# For Your Reference

# Biographical Dictionary

The Biographical Dictionary lists many of the important people introduced in this book. The page number tells where the main discussion of each person starts. See the Index for other page references.

**Addams, Jane** (1860–1935)  American who started Hull-House to help poor people in Chicago. p. 207

**Aesop**  Greek who told fables that children still enjoy today. p. 150

**Austin, Stephen F.** (1793–1836) American who started a colony in Texas. p. 189

**Barton, Clara** (1821–1912)  Founder of the American Red Cross. She was its first president. p. 69

**Bell, Alexander Graham** (1847–1922) American who invented the telephone. He also trained teachers to help people with hearing losses. p. 216

**Bellamy, Francis** (1855–1931)  American minister. He wrote the Pledge of Allegiance in 1892. p. 41

**Bethune, Mary McLeod** (1875–1955) African American teacher. Her work gave other African Americans the chance to go to school. p. 15

**Bush, George W.** (1946– )  43rd President of the United States. His father was 41st President. p. 54

**Carver, George Washington** (1864–1943)  African American scientist. His work helped farmers grow better crops. p. 208

**Clemente, Roberto** (1934–1972) Famous Puerto Rican baseball player who helped many people. p. 209

**Columbus, Christopher** (1451–1506) Italian explorer who sailed to the Americas. p. 194

**Douglas, Marjory Stoneman** (1890–1998)  American writer. She worked to protect the Florida Everglades. p. 115

**Edison, Thomas** (1847–1931)  American inventor. He invented the lightbulb and many other things. p. 211

**Franklin, Benjamin** (1706–1790) American leader, writer, and inventor. He helped write the Declaration of Independence. p. 206

**Hale, Nathan** (1755–1776)  American hero who was captured by the British. p. 68

**Houston, Sam** (1793–1863)  American who led Texas in its fight for independence. p. 69

**Jefferson, Thomas** (1743–1826)  Third President of the United States. He was the main writer of the Declaration of Independence. p. 57

**Jones, John Paul** (1747–1792) Commander of the American Navy in the Revolutionary War. p. 206

**King, Martin Luther, Jr.** (1929–1968) African American minister and leader. He worked to win civil rights for all Americans. p. 200

**Kwolek, Stephanie** (1923– ) American inventor. She found a way to make a cloth that is stronger than steel. p. 70

**Lincoln, Abraham** (1809–1865) 16th President of the United States. He made it against the law to own slaves. p. 201

**O'Connor, Sandra Day** (1930– ) First female Justice of the United States Supreme Court. p. 209

**Ochoa, Ellen** (1955– ) American astronaut. She was the first Hispanic female to go into space. p. 257

**Oglethorpe, James** (1696–1785) English settler who started the colony of Georgia. p. 189

**Penn, William** (1644–1718) English settler who started the colony of Pennsylvania. p. 188

**Pitcher, Molly** (1754?–1832) Nickname of Mary Hays McCauly. She brought pitchers of water to soldiers in the Revolutionary War. p. 207

**Roosevelt, Eleanor** (1884–1962) President Franklin Roosevelt's wife. She worked to make things better for the poor and for children. p. 70

**Sequoyah** (1765?–1843) Cherokee leader. He created a way to write the Cherokee language. p. 207

**Wagner, Honus** (1874–1955) One of the greatest baseball players in history. He played shortstop. p. 269

**Washington, George** (1732–1799) First President of the United States. He is known as "The Father of Our Country." p. 56

**Wells, Ida B**. (1862–1931) African American newspaper writer. She helped get laws passed for the fair treatment of African Americans. p. 208

**Wheatley, Phillis** (1753?–1784) African American poet. p. 207

**Wright, Orville** (1871–1948) and **Wilbur** (1867–1912) First Americans to fly a motor-powered airplane. p. 208

# Picture Glossary

## A

### address
The numbers and words that tell where a building is. (page 84)

### border

A line on a map that shows where a state or country ends. (page 52)

## B

### ballot
A piece of paper that shows the choices for voting. (page 58)

### business

The making or selling of goods or services. (page 252)

### bar graph
A graph that uses bars to show how many or how much. (page 262)

## C

### calendar
A chart that shows the days, weeks, and months in a year. (page 158)

**284**

**cause**
What makes
something happen.
(page 190)

**citizen**
A person who lives
in and belongs to a
community. (page 68)

**celebration**
A time to be happy
about something
special. (page 154)

**city**
A very large town.
(page 50)

**change**
To become different.
(page 175)

**communication**
The sharing of ideas
and information.
(page 214)

**community**
A group of people who live or work together. (page 46)

**culture**
A group's way of life. (page 143)

**continent**
One of the seven main land areas on Earth. (page 105)

**custom**
A group's way of doing something. (page 160)

**country**
An area of land with its own people and laws. (page 52)

**desert**
A large, dry area of land. (page 119)

**286**

I have a pet cat.

Her name is Snowball.

She is white.

**detail**
An extra piece of information about something. (page 8)

**distance**
How far one place is from another. (page 152)

**diagram**
A drawing that shows parts of something. (page 182)

E

**Earth**
Our planet. (page 104)

**direction**
The way to go to find something. (page 106)

**effect**
What happens because of a cause. (page 190)

**explorer**
A person who goes first to find out about a place. (page 194)

**factory**
A building in which people use machines to make goods. (page 244)

**fable**
A made-up story that teaches a lesson. (page 150)

**fair**
Done in a way that is right and honest. (page 11)

Fact The Liberty Bell cracked in 1835.

**fact**
A piece of information that is true. (page 66)

**farm**
A place where crops are grown and animals are raised for food. (page 108)

**288**

**fiction**
Stories that are made up. (page 66)

**freedom**
The right of people to make their own choices. (page 199)

**flag**
A piece of cloth with a special design that stands for a country or group. (page 62)

**future**
The time that is to come. (page 186)

**forest**
A very large area of trees. (page 109)

**globe**
A model of Earth. (page 104)

**goods**
Things that can be bought and sold. (page 240)

**group**
A number of people working together. (page 12)

**government**
The group of citizens that runs a community, state, or country. (page 51)

**hero**
A person who has done something brave or important. (page 206)

**governor**
The leader of a state's government. (page 51)

**hill**
Land that rises above the land around it. (page 100)

**290**

**history**
The story of what has happened in the past. (page 178)

**lake**
A body of water that has land all around it. (page 99)

**holiday**
A day to celebrate or remember something. (page 154)

**language**
The words or signs people use to communicate. (page 132)

**island**
A piece of land that has water all around it. (page 101)

**law**
A rule that people in a community must follow. (page 46)

**leader**
A person who helps a group plan what to do. (page 48)

**location**
The place where something is. (page 18)

**learn**
To find out something new. (page 6)

**main idea**
What the information that you are reading is mostly about. (page 8)

**litter**
To leave trash on the ground. (page 115)

**map**
A drawing that shows where places are. (page 20)

**map key**
The part of a map that shows what the symbols mean. (page 96)

**mayor**
The leader of a city or town government. (page 50)

**map scale**
The part of a map that helps you find the distance between two places. (page 152)

**money**
The coins and paper bills used to buy things. (page 252)

**market**
A place where people buy and sell goods. (page 258)

**mountain**
The highest kind of land. (page 98)

**N**

**needs**
Things people must have to live. (page 138)

**neighborhood**
The part of a community in which a group of people lives. (page 94)

**nonfiction**
Stories that have real information. (page 66)

**O**

**ocean**
A very large body of salty water. (page 105)

**P**

**past**
The time before now. (page 184)

**peace**
A time of quietness and calm. (page 203)

## picture graph
A graph that uses pictures to stand for numbers of things. (page 250)

## pollution
Anything that makes the air, land, or water dirty. (page 114)

## plain
Land that is mostly flat. (page 100)

## predict
To say what will happen. (page 112)

## point of view
A way of thinking about something. (page 146)

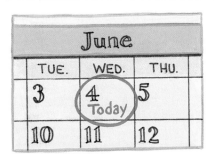

## present
The time now. (page 186)

**President**
Leader of the United States government. (page 54)

**recreation**
The things people do in their spare time, such as playing sports or having hobbies. (page 215)

**principal**
The leader of a school. (page 14)

**recycle**
To use things again. (page 117)

**problem**
Something that causes trouble. (page 136)

**religion**
A belief in a god or gods. (page 144)

**resource**
Anything that people can use. (page 108)

**river**
A stream of water that flows across the land. (page 101)

**responsibility**
Something that a citizen should do. (page 73)

**robot**
A machine run by a computer to do work. (page 257)

**right**
A freedom. (page 72)

**role**
The part a person plays in a group or community. (page 134)

**route**
A way to go from
one place to another.
(page 204)

**scarce**
Not in good supply,
or hard to find.
(page 266)

**rule**
An instruction
telling what must or
must not be done.
(page 10)

**school**
A place where
people go to learn.
(page 4)

**save**
To keep something,
such as money, to
use later. (page 260)

**season**
One of the four parts
of the year that have
different kinds of
weather. (page 175)

**services**
Work done for others for money. (page 242)

**shelter**
A safe place to live. (page 138)

**settler**
One of the first people to make a home in a new place. (page 196)

**solution**
The answer to a problem. (page 136)

**share**
To tell others what we know or think. (page 7)

**state**
A part of a country. (page 52)

**symbol**
A picture or object that stands for something else. (page 20)

**technology**
New inventions that we use in everyday life. (page 210)

**table**
A chart that shows information in rows and columns. (page 28)

**time line**
A line that shows when events happened. (page 176)

**teacher**
A person who helps others learn. (page 14)

**today**
This day. (page 174)

**300**

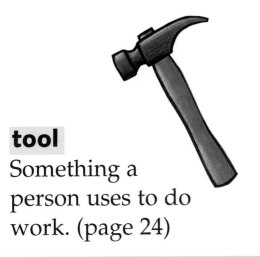

**tomorrow**
The day after today.
(page 174)

**transportation**
Ways of carrying
people and goods
from one place to
another. (page 212)

**V**

**tool**
Something a
person uses to do
work. (page 24)

**valley**
Low land between
mountains. (page 98)

**trade**
To give one thing to
get another. (page 268)

**veteran**
A person who has
served in the
military. (page 203)

**volunteer**
A person who works
without being paid.
(page 253)

**weather**
What the air outside
is like. (page 112)

**vote**
A choice that gets
counted. (page 58)

**world**
All the people
and places on Earth.
(page 30)

W

**wants**
Things that people
would like to have
but do not need.
(page 264)

Y

**yesterday**
The day before
today. (page 174)

# Index

INDEX

**D**

**E**

**F**

INDEX

INDEX

**308**

For permission to reprint copyrighted material, grateful acknowledgment is made to the following sources:

*Atheneum Books for Young Readers, an imprint of Simon & Schuster Children's Publishing Division:* Cover illustration by Barry Root from *Messenger, Messenger* by Robert Burleigh. Illustration copyright © 2000 by Barry Root.

*Curtis Brown, Ltd.:* "School Bus" from *School Supplies: A Book of Poems* by Lee Bennett Hopkins. Text copyright © 1996 by Lee Bennett Hopkins. Published by Simon & Schuster Books for Young Readers.

*Marc Brown Studios:* From *Arthur Meets the President* by Marc Brown. Copyright © 1991 by Marc Brown. Published by Little, Brown and Company (Inc.).

*Charlesbridge Publishing, Inc.:* Cover illustration by Ralph Masiello from *The Flag We Love* by Pam Muñoz Ryan. Illustration copyright © 1996 by Ralph Masiello.

*Children's Press, a Division of Grolier Publishing:* From *George Washington: First President of the United States* by Carol Greene. Copyright © 1991 by Childrens Press®, Inc.

*Chronicle Books, San Francisco:* Cover illustration by Donna Ingemanson from *Something's Happening on Calabash Street* by Judith Ross Enderle and Stephanie Jacob Gordon. Illustration copyright © 2000 by Donna Ingemanson.

*Cobblehill Books, an affiliate of Dutton Children's Books, a division of Penguin Putnam Inc.:* Cover photographs from *Emeka's Gift: An African Counting Story* by Ifeoma Onyefulu. Photographs copyright © 1995 by Ifeoma Onyefulu.

*Crown Children's Books, a division of Random House, Inc.:* Cover illustration by Annette Cable from *Me On the Map* by Joan Sweeney. Illustration copyright © 1996 by Annette Cable.

*Farrar, Straus and Giroux, LLC:* Cover illustration from *Madlenka* by Peter Sis. Copyright © 2000 by Peter Sis.

*Harcourt, Inc.:* Cover illustration from *Market Day* by Lois Ehlert. Copyright © 2000 by Lois Ehlert. Cover illustration from *Check It Out! The Book About Libraries* by Gail Gibbons. Copyright © 1985 by Gail Gibbons.

*HarperCollins Publishers:* Cover illustration by Diane Greenseid from *Get Up and Go!* by Stuart J. Murphy. Illustration copyright © 1996 by Diane Greenseid.

*Holiday House, Inc.:* Cover illustration from *First Day, Hooray!* by Nancy Poydar. Copyright © 1999 by Nancy Poydar.

*Henry Holt and Company, LLC:* From *Here to There* by Margery Cuyler, illustrated by Yu Cha Pak. Text copyright © 1999 by Margery Cuyler; illustrations copyright © 1999 by Yu Cha Pak.

*Houghton Mifflin Company:* Cover illustration by Arthur Geisert from *Haystack* by Bonnie Geisert. Illustration copyright © 1995 by Arthur Geisert. From *Rush Hour* by Christine Loomis, illustrated by Mari Takabayashi. Text copyright © 1996 by Christine Loomis; illustrations copyright © 1996 by Mari Takabayashi.

*Little, Brown and Company (Inc.):* "Four Generations" from *Fathers, Mothers, Sisters, Brothers: A Collection of Family Poems* by Mary Ann Hoberman. Text copyright © 1991 by Mary Ann Hoberman.

*The Millbrook Press:* Cover illustration by Anca Hariton from *Compost! Growing Gardens from Your Garbage* by Linda Glaser. Illustration copyright © 1996 by Anca Hariton.

*Scholastic Inc.:* Cover illustration by Nila Aye from *When I'm Big* by Tim Drury. Illustration copyright © 1999 by Nila Aye. Published by Orchard Books, an imprint of Scholastic Inc.

*SeaStar Books, a division of North-South Books, Inc., New York:* Cover illustration from *The Inside-Outside Book of Washington, D.C.* by Roxie Munro. Copyright © 1987, 2001 by Roxie Munro.

*Simon & Schuster Books for Young Readers, an imprint of Simon & Schuster Children's Publishing Division:* Cover illustration by Michael P. Paraskevas from *On the Day the Tall Ships Sailed* by Betty Paraskevas. Illustration copyright © 2000 by Michael P. Paraskevas.

*Walker and Company:* Cover illustration by Eric Velasquez from *The Piano Man* by Debbi Chocolate. Illustration copyright © 1998 by Eric Velasquez.

*Albert Whitman & Company:* Cover illustration by Paige Billin-Frye from *This Is the Turkey* by Abby Levine. Illustration copyright © 2000 by Paige Billin-Frye. Cover illustration by DyAnne DiSalvo-Ryan from *If I Were President* by Catherine Stier. Illustration copyright © 1999 by DyAnne DiSalvo-Ryan.

**PHOTO CREDITS:**
**KEY: (T)-TOP; (B)-BOTTOM; (L)-LEFT; (R)-RIGHT; (C)-CENTER; (BG)-BACKGROUND; (FG)-FOREGROUND**

**FRONT TITLE PAGE**

Front Side: (fg) Minden Pictures; (bg) Don Mason/Corbis Stock Market; Back Side: (bg) Don Mason/Corbis Stock Market

**TITLE PAGE AND TABLE OF CONTENTS:**

i (fg) Shelburne Museum; i (bg) Doug Armand/Stone; ii (bl) Shelburne Museum; iv (cl) Shelburne Museum; v (tl) Newlab; viii (tl) Erich Lessing/Art Resource; ix (tl) Smithsonian Institution

**UNIT 1:**

Opener: (fg) Shelburne Museum; 1 (tc) Shelburne Museum; 2 (cr) Ellen Senisi/The Image Works, Inc.; 3 (tr) Superstock; 3 (b) Bob Daemmrich/Stock, Boston; 9 (t) J.C. Carton/Bruce Coleman, Inc.; 14 (b) Bob Daemmrich Photography; 15 (t) Jim Pickerell/Stock Connection/PictureQuest; 15 (b) Gordon Parks/Hulton/Archive Photos; 16 (t) L. O'Shaughnessy/H. Armstrong Roberts; 17 (t) Bob Daemmrich Photography; 18 (b) Peter Cade/Stone; 22 (c) Jeff Greenberg/Stock, Boston; 22 (c) Mark E. Gibson Photography; 23 (c) Richard T. Nowitz; 23 (bl) West Sedona School; 23 (br) James Marshall/The Image Works; 24 (t,c & bl) Blackwell History of Education Museum; 25 (b) Jack McConnell/McConnell & McNamara; 25 (tl) Gloria Rejune Adams/Old School Square; 26 (tl) Brent Jones/Stock, Boston; 26 (br) Michael Newman/PhotoEdit/PictureQuest; 28 (t) Blackwell History of Education Museum; 29 (cl, bl & tl) Blackwell History of Education Museum; 29 (bcl) Gloria Rejune Adams/Old School Square; 30 (cr) G. Popov/Sovfoto/Eastfoto/PictureQuest; 30 (cl) Bob Daemmrich Photography/Stock, Boston; 31 (br) Jay Ireland & Georgienne E. Bradley/Bradleyireland.com; 31(cr) Nicholas DeVore, III/Bruce Coleman, Inc.; 31(cl) Sheila McKinnon/Mira; 32 (t) Victor Englebert; 32 (bl) Burbank/The Image Works; 33 (c) D. Donadoni/Bruce Coleman, Inc.; 34-35 (all) Photopia

**UNIT 2**

Opener: (fg) Newlab; (bg) Robert Frerck/Odyssey Productions, Chicago; 41 (tc) Newlab; 42 (tl) David Young-Wolff/PhotoEdit/PictureQuest; 43 (tl) Reuters NewMedia/Corbis; 43 (bl) B. Daemmrich/The Image Works; 43 (cr) John Henry Williams/Bruce Coleman, Inc.; 46 (c) Alan Schein/Corbis Stock Market; 46 (br) DiMaggio/Kalish/Corbis Stock Market; 46 (cr) Joe Sohm/Pictor; 47 (c) ©Diane M. Meyer; 49 (t) Ken Chernus/FPG International; 49 (cl) PhotoDisc/Getty Images; 50-51 (all) David R. Frazier; 52 (br) Michael Hubrich/Photo Researchers; 52 (bg) Corel Collection, 1993; 54 (b) MIA/TimePix; 55 (t) Time For Kids Magazine; 55 (bl) Reuters/TimePix; 55 (br) Tim Sloan/Corbis; 55 (cr) Robert Essel/Corbis Stock Market; 56 (bc) Peggy and Ronald Barnett/Corbis Stock Market; 56 (cr) Visions of America; 60 (c) Frank Oberle/Stone; 60 (b) Phil Degginger/Color-Pic, Inc.; 61 (tl) Kunio Owaki/Corbis Stock Market; 61 (tr) Ed Wheeler/Corbis Stock Market; 61 (bl) B. Bachmann/The Image Works, Inc.; 61 (br) Joe Sohm/Visions of America; 61(cl) D. Boone/Corbis; 63 (t) Joe Sohm/Visions of America; 63 (cl) Bob Daemmrich/The Image Works, Inc.; 64 (b) Joe Sohm/Visions of America; 65 (cl) The Granger Collection; 66 (t) Grolier Publishing; 66 (b) Grolier Publishing; 68 (bl) The Antiquarian & Landmarks Society; 68 (cr) Joe Sohm/Visions of America; 69 (tl) Hulton Archive; 69 (bl) National Archives; 69 (br) Joe Sohm/Visions of America; 70 (t) Bettmann/Corbis; 70 (bl) Courtesy of DuPont; 70 (br) Color-Pic, Inc./E.R. Degginger; 71 (c) Anton Oparin/Corbis SABA; 72 (bl) PictureQuest; 72 (br) Bob Daemmrich/Stock, Boston/PictureQuest; 73 (tl) Michael Newman/PhotoEdit; 73 (cr) Photodisc; 74 (b) Larry Evans/Black Star; 74 (cr) Bettmann/Corbis; 75 (c) Larry Evans/Black Star; 75 (tc) Public Art Program/Chicago Cultural Center; 75 (tr) Chicago Historical Society; 75 (bl) Todd Buchanan/Black Star; 75 (cr) Hulton-Deutsch Collection/Corbis

**UNIT 3**

Opener: (bg) Mark E. Gibson; 82 (tl) Richard Pasley/Stock, Boston; 82 (br) Nigel Press/Stone; 83 (tl) Buddy Mays/Travel Stock; 83 (bl) W. Perry Conway/Corbis; 83 (br) R. Walker/H. Armstrong Roberts, Inc.; 94 (b) Bob Daemmrich Photography; 96 (b) Robert Winslow/The Viesti Collection; 98 (bc) Superstock; 98-99 (bg) Superstock; 99 (b) Joseph R. Melanson/Aerials Only Gallery/Aero Photo; 99 (cl) U. S. Postal Services; 100 (both) Superstock; 101 (tc) T. Dickinson/The Image Works; 101 (tr) U.S. Postal Services; 101 (cr)Robert Winslow/The Viesti Collection; 102-103 (b) Dick Dietrich; 108 (bl) Bruce Hands/Stone; 108-109 (bg) John Lawrence/Stone; 109 (tr) Fred Habegger/Grant Heilman Photography; 109 (cr & br) B. Daemmrich/The Image Works; 110 (bl) Mark E. Gibson Photography; 111 (tr) David Young-Wolff/PhotoEdit; 111 (br) Bob Daemmrich/The Image Works; 111 (bg) Jan Butchofsky-Houser/Houserstock; 111 (cl) Jim Nilsen/Stone; 112 (b) A. & J. Verkaik/Corbis Stock Market; 113 (c) Larry Lefever/Grant Heilman Photography; 114 (b) Dan Guravich/Corbis; 114-115 (bg) Randy

Wells Photography; 115 (cr) Kevin Fleming/Corbis; 116 (tr) Geri Engberg Photography; 117 (cl) Mark E. Gibson Photography; 118 (c & br) Superstock; 118 (bg) Buddy Mays/Travel Stock Photography; 119 (tr) W. Jacobs/Art Directors & TRIP Photo Library; 119 (tr) Jay Ireland & Georgienne E. Bradley/Bradleyireland.com; 119 (bl) Inger Hogstrom/Danita Delimont, Agent; 119 (cl) K. Rice/H. Armstrong Roberts, Inc.; 120 (b) Superstock; 120 (tr) Siede Preis/PhotoDisc/PictureQuest; 121 (tc) Superstock; 121 (tr) Sami Sarkis/Getty Images/PhotoDisc; 121 (bc) PhotoDisc/Getty Images; 121 (cl) Wolfgang Kaehler Photography; 122 (tr) Ian Adams/Garden Image; 122 (bl) Sara Demmons; 122 (cr) Laurie Dove/Garden Image; 123 (tr) Phillip Roullard/Garden Image; 123 (tl, bl & cl) Judith Lindsey; 123 (cr) Woodbridge Williams/Garden Image

**UNIT 4**

30 (tl) Norbert Schafer/Corbis Stock Market; 131 (tl) Lee Snider/The Image Works; 131 (tr) Bachmann/Unicorn Stock Photos; 131 (bl) Bob Daemmrich/Stock, Boston; 132 (bl) Marilyn "Angel" Wynn/Nativestock.com; 132 (br & t) Melanie Weiner Photography; 133 (c) Photodisc; 140 (tr) H.Thomas III/Unicorn Stock Photos; 140 (bl) Bob Daemmrich/The Image Works, Inc.; 140 (br) Dave Bartruf/Corbis; 140 (cl) John Elk III; 141 (b & tr) Topham/The Image Works; 141 (tl) Eric Crichton/Bruce Coleman, Inc.; 142 (cr) Ted Streshinsky/Corbis; 143 (tr) Superstock; 143 (bc) Momatiuk Eastcott/The Image Works; 143 (cl) Susan Lapides/Woodfin Camp & Associates; 144 (tl) Hanan Isachar/www.holylandiamges.com; 144 (tr) Christine Osborne Pictures; 144 (bc) Macduff Everton/The Image Works; 144 (br) David R. Frazier; 148 (bl)The Newark Museum/Art Resource, NY; 148 (cr) Corbis; 149 (t) C Squared Studios/PhotoDisc/PictureQuest; 149 (bl) Bowers Museum of Cultural Arts/Corbis; 149 (br) Lawrence Migdale; 149 (cr) Mimmo Jodice/Corbis; 150 (cl) The University of Southern Mississippi; 151 (cl) Courtesy of Michigan State University/Feldman & Associates; 151 (cr) UCLA Fowler Museum of Cultural Arts, photograph by Don Cole; 154 (all) Superstock; 155 (tc) Ray Morsch/Corbis; 155 (tr) H. Rogers/Art Directors & TRIP Photo Library; 155 (bl) Suzanne Murphy/DDB Stock Photo; 155 (br) Alyx Kellington/DDB Stock Photo; 156 (tr) Billy Hustace/Stone; 156 (br) Paul Barton/Corbis Stock Market; 156 (cl) Kathy McLaughlin/The Image Works; 157 (tl) Richard T. Nowitz/Folio; 157 (tr) Ray Juno/Corbis Stock Market; 160 (cr) Bob Krist/PictureQuest; 160 (cl) Joe Sohm/Chromosohm/The Image Works; 161 (c) Tom & Dee Ann McCarthy/Corbis Stock Market; 161 (tr) Tony Freeman/PhotoEdit; 162 (all) The Institute of Texan Cultures

**UNIT 5**

Opener: (fg) Erich Lessing/Art Resource; 169 (tc) Erich Lessing/Art Resource; 170 (tl) S.A. Kraulis/Masterfile; 170 (bl) 2001 by the New York Times Co. Reprinted by permission. 1927; 170 (cr) Jon Gnass/Gnass Photo Images; 171 (bl) Paul Barton/Corbis Stock Market; 171 (cr) Science Photo Library/Photo Researchers; 175 (tl) Superstock; 175 (tr) Mark E. Gibson;175 (cl) Rommel/Masterfile; 175 (cr) Superstock; 176 (bc) PhotoDisc; 178-179 (b) Sarah H. Cotter/Bruce Coleman, Inc.; 178 (cl & cr) PhotoDisc; 179 (c, bl & br) PhotoDisc; 181 (cl) Pat Lanza/Bruce Coleman, Inc.; 184-185 (all) North Carolina Collection, University of North Carolina Library at Chapel Hill; 186-187 (all) Kelly Culpepper; 188 (both) Historical Society of Pennsylvania; 189 (tl) Hulton/Archive; 189 (cr) Texas State Library & Archives Commission; 190-191 (t) Johnny Crawford/The Image Works; 191 (c) Kevin Horan/Stock, Boston Inc./PictureQuest; 194 (tr) Bettmann/Corbis; 196 (b) Bert Lane/Plimoth Plantation; 197 (both) Ted Curtin/Plimoth Plantation;198 (c) George F. Mobley/Courtesy U.S. Capitol Historical Society; 198 (b) Joseph Sohm/Corbis; 198 (tr) Peggy & Ronald Barnett/Corbis Stock Market; 199 (tr) Joe Sohm/Photo Researchers; 200 (t) Hulton-Deutsch Collection/Corbis; 201 (tr) United States Postal Service; 201 (br) Denise Cupen/Bruce Coleman, Inc.; 202 (c) James P. Blair/Corbis; 202 (b) Frank Siteman/Stock, Boston; 202 (tl) United States Postal Service; 202 (tr) John Neubauer/PhotoEdit; 202 (cl & cr) United States Postal Service; 203 (c) Joe Sohm/ChromoSohm Media; 203 (tr) National Archives; 208 (both) Bettman/Corbis; 209 (c) Bettman/Corbis; 209 (tr) Reuters NewMedia, Inc./Corbis; 210 (bl) Anthony Meshkinyar/Stone; 210 (br) Michael Boys/Corbis; 211 (c) H.H. Thomas/Unicorn Stock Photos; 211 (tc) Phyllis Kedl/Unicorn Stock Photos; 211 (tr) Anthony Marsland/Stone; 211 (br) Corbis; 211 (cl) PictureQuest; 212-213 (t) D. & J. Heaton/Stock, Boston; 212 (c) Chad Slattery/Stone; 212 (tl) Philip Wallick/Corbis Stock Market; 212 (bl) AFP/Corbis; 212 (br) Superstock; 213 (c) Leo de Wys Photo Agency/eStock Photography/PictureQuest; 213 (b) Torleif Svensson/Corbis Stock Market; 213 (tc) Superstock; 213 (bl) Stone; 213 (cr) Brian K. Miller/Bruce Coleman, Inc.; 214 (c) D. Young-Wolff/PhotoEdit; 214 (tl) Topham/The Image Works; 214 (tc) Archivo Iconografico, S.A./Corbis; 214 (bc) Don Mason/Corbis Stock Market; 214 (br) NASA; 214 (cl) John Elk III/Stock, Boston; 215 (c) Chris Hellier/Corbis; 215 (c) L. Hafencher/H. Armstrong Roberts; 215 (tc) Rudi Von Briel; 215 (tr) DiMaggio/Kalish/Corbis Stock Market; 216 (bl) Underwood & Underwood/Corbis; 216 (br) The Museum of Independent Telephony; 216 (cr) Corbis; 217 (tl) The Museum of Independent Telephny; 217 (tr) Superstock; 218 (bl, br, cl & cr) Thomas Neill/Old Sturbridge Village; 224 (both) Stephen F. Austin State University

**UNIT 6**

Opener: (fg) Smithsonian Institution; (bg) Nick Gunderson/Stone; 225 (tc) Smithsonian Institution; 226 (tl) Burke/Triolo/Brand X Pictures/PictureQuest; 226 (br) Mark E. Gibson Photography; 227 (tl) Bob Donaldson/Pittsburgh Post-Gazette; 227 (bl) David Young-Wolff/PhotoEdit; 227 (cr) Syracuse Newspaper/Katie Ciccarello/The Image Works, Inc.; 240 (b) Aneal S. Vohra/Unicorn Stock Photos; 241 (tl) Ariel Skelley/Corbis Stock Market; 241 (tr) Michael Newman/PhotoEdit; 241 (br) Christopher Bissell/Stone; 241 (bg) PhotoDisc/Getty Images; 241 (cr) Hans Reinhard/Bruce Coleman, Inc.; 242 (tl) Bob Daemmrich/The Image Works; 242 (bl) Dan Bosler/Stone; 242 (cr) Aaron Haupt/Photo Researchers, Inc.; 243 (tr) Steven Peters/Stone; 243 (cl) Richard Hutchings/Photo Researchers; 244 (b) Richard Hutchings Photography; 245 (c) Art Directors & TRIP Photo Library; 245 (cr) Bob Clay/Visuals Unlimited; 246-248 (all) Richard Hutchings Photography; 253 (c) Hans Reinhard/Bruce Coleman Collection; 254 (bl) Burke/Triolo/Brand X Pictures/PictureQuest; 254 (bc) H. Armstrong Roberts/Corbis Stock Market; 255 (tl) Spencer Grant/PhotoEdit; 255 (tr & bl) Hulton/Archive Photos; 256 (tr) Bettmann/Corbis; 256 (bl) Pittsburgh Post-Gazette; 256 (br & cl) Hulton/Archive Photos; 257 (tl) Ray Juno/Corbis Stock Market; 257 (tr) NASA; 257 (cr) Agence France Presse/Corbis; 257 (cl) Doug Martin/Photo Researchers, Inc.; 258-259 (bg) Van Bucher/Photo Researchers; 262 (b) Morton Beebe, S.F./Corbis; 264 (br) Superstock; 264 (bg) Don Mason/Corbis Stock Market; 267 (cr) Anthony Meshkinyar/Stone; 268 (b) Esbian Anderson/The Image Works; 270 (b) Donnezan/Explorer/Photo Researchers, Inc.; 272 (tr) David R. Frazier; 273 (t) George Hall/Corbis; 273 (b) Stephen Kline/Bruce Coleman, Inc.; 274 (tr) Carlo Hindian/Masterfile; 274 (bl) Jef Zaruba/Corbis; 274 (br) Sven Martson/The Image Works; 275 (tl) Bob Daemmrich/Stock, Boston; 275 (tr) Rolf Bruderer/Corbis Stock Market; 275 (bl) John Lei/Stock, Boston; 275 (cl) Michael Philip Manheim/The Image Finders

All other photos from Harcourt School Photo Library and Photographers: Weronica Ankarorn, Victoria Bowen, Ken Kinzie, Quebecor World Imaging.